A Newman Reader

A Newman Reader

Matthew Muller, Ph.D., Editor

Our Sunday Visitor
Huntington, Indiana

This book is dedicated to my children,
Anthony, Owen, and Juliana. *Cor ad cor loquitor.*

Our Sunday Visitor Publishing Division
Our Sunday Visitor, Inc.
200 Noll Plaza
Huntington, IN 46750
www.osv.com
1-800-348-2440

ISBN: 978-1-68192-618-6 (Inventory No. T2481)
1. RELIGION—Christianity—Saints & Sainthood. 2. RELIGION—Christian Theology—General. 3. RELIGION—Christianity—Catholic.

eISBN: 978-1-68192-619-3
LCCN: 2019950126

Cover design: Lindsey Riesen
Cover art: Cardinal Newman, 1887 (b/w photo), Barraud, Herbert Rose (1845-c.1896) / Private Collection / Bridgeman Images
Interior design: Amanda Falk

PRINTED IN THE UNITED STATES OF AMERICA

Contents

Letters

Introduction

By Matthew Muller Ph.D.

Saint John Henry Newman is well known today as a convert and intellectual, but he was first and foremost a disciple of Christ and a pastor, selecting as his cardinalate motto, *Cor ad cor loquitor*, heart speaks to heart. He cared deeply for the spiritual wellbeing of his students and parishioners at Oxford University. From the Birmingham Oratory he worked tirelessly for the spiritual good of English Catholics and for the evangelization of his home country. He challenged his flock, and he challenges us today to be well-formed in order to be able to "give an account" of the Catholic Faith. He said,

> You must not hide your talent in a napkin, or
> your light under a bushel. I want a laity [...] who
> know their religion, who enter into it, who know
> just where they stand, who know what they hold,

> and what they do not, who know their creed so
> well, that they can give an account of it, who
> know so much of history that they can defend it.
> I want an intelligent, well-instructed laity.[1]

As a pastor, Newman spent a great deal of time as a preacher. His sermons are timeless classics of Catholic spirituality. Adamantly opposed to emotionally charged preaching that sought conversion through powerful style and delivery, Newman sought to move his audiences through the power of his words and imagery. Despite his slow, quiet, and deliberate style, people hung on his words. In his preaching he combined a mastery of Sacred Scripture with spiritual wisdom and insight. He knew how the human heart seeks its own ways, and he called it back to loving obedience to Christ. For the Church today, his sermons penetrate the thin shell of our comfortable lives, calling us out of our worldliness to live a life focused on total love of God.

Newman was born in London, England, on February 21, 1801, and he died at the Birmingham Oratory on August 11, 1890. He was an intellectual and spiritual giant of the Victorian era, and his vast body of writings and letters are classic examples of the character of his age. The first half of his life was spent as an Anglican at Oxford University, where he helped to launch the Oxford Movement, an attempt at a *via media*, a middle way between Roman Catholicism and Protestantism that advocated for a return to tradition, sacramental worship, imagination, and ecclesial authority. After his conversion to Catholicism in 1845, the next half of his life was spent as an Oratorian in Birmingham, England. Throughout his life, even after his conversion, Newman endured obstacles, suspicion, and calumny. For some he was too liberal, for others he was too conservative. But he received validation of

---

1. *On the Present Position of Catholics in England*, 390 (1851). All citations of Newman's works are taken from editions available at www.newmanreader.org.

his career when Pope Leo XIII named him a cardinal in 1879. His enduring trust in God's providence amidst trials is the source of his saintliness and an inspiration for the Church today.

Newman is most well-known as a convert to Catholicism. He famously wrote, "To be deep in history is to cease to be a Protestant."[2] Prior to his conversion, he was at the peak of his career in the Church of England. He left behind income, status, and friendships to follow the Truth. The Truth led him into a Church deeply despised by many of his own countrymen. It was a profound act of faith, hope, and love, which inspired many other conversions in England and beckons us today to put love of Christ above the things of the world.

Even though he was a musician, poet, historian, philosopher, and theologian, Newman described himself as a controversialist. He never wrote without some question or provocation before him. Controversy brought out the best of his unique blend of intellectual power and rhetorical skill. His most influential works, *An Essay on the Development of Christian Doctrine* (1845), *The Idea of a University* (1858), *Apologia pro vita sua* (1864), and *An Essay in Aid of a Grammar of Assent* (1870), were written to respond to immediate needs, but have enduring relevance.

As a theologian, Newman's writings on the development of doctrine and on the importance of conscience have had a lasting impact on Catholic theology. He wrote his essay on development of doctrine on the eve of his conversion to Catholicism, knowing he would have to give an account of his decision. It is arguably his most important contribution to Catholic theology, impacting the decisions of the Council Fathers at Vatican I and Vatican II. Later, after Vatican I defined papal infallibility, Newman wrote on the importance of conscience in his "Letter to the Duke of Norfolk." His teachings on the freedom of conscience are an important cor-

---

2. Essay on the Development of Christian Doctrine, 8 (1878).

rective to our relativistic sense of freedom and individual liberty.

Education also played a major role in Newman's life and work. His reputation and experience as a fellow of Oriel College at Oxford University led the bishops of Ireland to invite him to help found the first Catholic university in Ireland. For many reasons, most of which were outside of Newman's control, the project failed. However, it led him to write *The Idea of a University*, which remains essential reading for anyone concerned with the integration of faith and reason within education.

Newman was also engaged in some of the major philosophical questions of his day, especially Enlightenment critiques of the reasonableness of faith. He showed that belief is a necessary component for life and demonstrated the coherence of belief in Christ and the teachings of the Church. His book, *An Essay in Aid of a Grammar of Assent*, is one of his most challenging works, and it remains an extremely important contribution to defending the rationality of faith to a secular, technocratic age.

Now the Church has the great blessing of knowing that Newman is a saint. He anticipated that Christianity in the age to come would experience many trials and tribulations, but he was also versed enough in Church history not to despair. Many times in her long history, the Church has faced scandal, persecution, corruption, and desolation, but Newman had hope because he knew that in each age the Lord raises up new saints. For the Church today, Newman proposed the example of Saint Philip Neri for the evangelization of culture. Saint Philip, Newman wrote, "preferred to yield to the stream, and direct the current, which he could not stop ... and to sweeten and to sanctify what God had made very good and man had spoilt."[3] Newman did this in his life, and he inspires us to do the same by living the truth in love, always prepared to give an account of the hope that is within us.[4]

---

3. *Idea of a University*, 235 (1873).
4. 1 Peter 3:15.

Essays

On the Introduction of Rationalistic Principles into Religion

#73 of Tracts for the Times (Excerpt) (1836)

1. Rationalism is a certain abuse of Reason; that is, a use of it for purposes for which it never was intended, and is unfitted. To rationalize in matters of Revelation is to make our reason the standard and measure of the doctrines revealed; to stipulate that those doctrines should be such as to carry with them their own justification; to reject them, if they come in collision with our existing opinions or habits of thought, or are with difficulty har-

monized with our existing stock of knowledge. And thus a rationalistic spirit is the antagonist of Faith; for Faith is, in its very nature, the acceptance of what our reason cannot reach, simply and absolutely upon testimony.

There is, of course, a multitude of cases in which we allowably and rightly accept statements as true, partly on reason, and partly on testimony. We supplement the information of others by our own knowledge, by our own judgment of probabilities; and, if it be very strange or extravagant, we suspend our assent. This is undeniable; still, after all, there are truths which are incapable of reaching us except on testimony, and there is testimony, which by and in itself, has an imperative claim on our acceptance.

As regards Revealed Truth, it is not Rationalism to set about to ascertain, by the exercise of reason, what things are attainable by reason, and what are not; nor, in the absence of an express Revelation, to inquire into the truths of Religion, as they come to us by nature; nor to determine what proofs are necessary for the acceptance of a Revelation, if it be given; nor to reject a Revelation on the plea of insufficient proof; nor, after recognizing it as divine, to investigate the meaning of its declarations, and to interpret its language; nor to use its doctrines, as far as they can be fairly used, in inquiring into its divinity; nor to compare and connect them with our previous knowledge, with a view of making them parts of a whole; nor to bring them into dependence on each other, to trace their mutual relations, and to pursue them to their legitimate issues. This is not Rationalism; but it is Rationalism to accept the Revelation, and then to explain it away; to speak of it as the Word of God, and to treat it as the word of man; to refuse to let it speak for itself; to claim to be told the *why* and the *how* of God's dealings with us, as therein described, and to assign to Him a motive and a scope of our own; to stumble at the partial knowledge which He may give us of them; to put aside what is obscure, as if it had not been said at all; to accept one half of what has been told us, and not the other half; to assume that the contents of Revelation are also its proof; to frame some gratuitous hypothesis about them, and then to garble, gloss, and color them, to trim, clip, pare away, and twist them, in order to bring them into conformity with the idea to which we have subjected them.

When the rich lord in Samaria said, "Though God shall make windows in heaven, shall this thing be?"[5] he rationalized, as professing his inability to discover *how* Elisha's prophecy was to be fulfilled, and thinking in this way to excuse his unbelief. When Naaman, after acknowledging the prophet's supernatural power, objected to bathe in Jordan, it was on the ground of his not seeing the *means* by which Jordan was to cure his leprosy above the rivers of Damascus.[6] "*How* can these things be?"[7] was the objection of Nicodemus to the doctrine of regeneration; and when the doctrine of the Holy Communion was first announced, "the Jews strove among themselves," in answer to their Divine Informant, saying, "*How* can this man give us His flesh to eat?"[8] When St. Thomas, believing in our Lord, doubted of our Lord's resurrection, though his reason for so doing is not given, it plainly lay in the astonishing, unaccountable nature of such an event. A like desire of judging for one's self is discernible in the original fall of man. Eve did not believe the Tempter, any more than God's word, till she perceived that "the fruit was good for food."

So again, when men who profess Christianity ask *how* prayer can really influence the course of God's providence, or *how* everlasting punishment, as such, consists with God's infinite mercy, they rationalize.

The same spirit shows itself in the restlessness of others to

---

5. 2 Kings 7:2.
6. 2 Kings 5.
7. John 3:9.
8. John 6:52.

decide *how* the sun was stopped at Joshua's word, *how* the manna was provided, and the like; forgetting what our Savior suggests to the Sadducees — "*the power* of God."[9]

2. Conduct such as this, on so momentous a matter, is, generally speaking, traceable to one obvious cause. The Rationalist makes himself his own center, not his Maker; he does not go to God, but he implies that God must come to him. And this, it is to be feared, is the spirit in which multitudes of us act at the present day. Instead of looking out of ourselves, and trying to catch glimpses of God's workings, from any quarter — throwing ourselves forward upon Him and waiting on Him, we sit at home bringing everything to ourselves, enthroning ourselves in our own views, and refusing to believe anything that does not force itself upon us as true. Our private judgment is made everything to us — is contemplated, recognized, and consulted as the arbiter of all questions, and as independent of everything external to us. Nothing is considered to have an existence except so far forth as our minds discern it. The notion of half views and partial knowledge, of guesses, surmises, hopes and fears, of truths faintly apprehended and not understood, of isolated facts in the great scheme of Providence, in a word, the idea of Mystery, is discarded.

Hence a distinction is drawn between what is called Objective and Subjective Truth, and Religion is said to consist in a reception of the latter. By Objective Truth is meant the Religious System considered as existing in itself, external to this or that particular mind: by Subjective, is meant that which each mind receives in particular, and considers to be such. To believe in Objective Truth is to throw ourselves forward upon that which we have but partially mastered or made subjective; to embrace, maintain, and use general propositions which are larger than our own capacity, of

---

9. Matthew 22:29.

which we cannot see the bottom, which we cannot follow out into their multiform details; to come before and bow before the import of such propositions, as if we were contemplating what is real and independent of human judgment. Such a belief, implicit, and symbolized as it is in the use of creeds, seems to the Rationalist superstitious and unmeaning, and he consequently confines Faith to the province of Subjective Truth, or to the reception of doctrine, as, and so far as, it is met and apprehended by the mind, which will be differently, as he considers, in different persons, in the shape of orthodoxy in one, heterodoxy in another. That is, he professes to *believe* in that which he *opines*; and he avoids the obvious extravagance of such an avowal by maintaining that the moral trial involved in Faith does not lie in the submission of the reason to external realities partially disclosed, but in what he calls that candid pursuit of truth which ensures the eventual adoption of that opinion on the subject, which is best for us individually, which is most natural according to the constitution of our own minds, and, therefore, divinely intended for us. I repeat, he owns that Faith, viewed with reference to its objects, is never more than an opinion, and is pleasing to God, not as an active principle apprehending definite doctrines, but as a result and fruit, and therefore an evidence of past diligence, independent inquiry, dispassionateness, and the like. Rationalism takes the words of Scripture as signs of Ideas; Faith, of Things or Realities.

For an illustration of Faith, considered as the reaching forth after and embracing what is beyond the mind, or Objective, we may refer to St. Paul's description of it in the ancient Saints: "These all died in Faith, *not having received* the promises, but *having seen them afar off*, and were persuaded of them, and embraced them, and confessed that they were strangers and pilgrims on the earth";[10] or to St. Peter's: "Of which salvation the

---

10. Hebrews 11:13.

Prophets have inquired and searched diligently, who *prophesied* of the grace that should come *unto you, searching what, or what manner of time* the Spirit of Christ which was in them did signify, when it testified beforehand the sufferings of Christ, and the glory that should follow; unto whom it was revealed, that *not unto themselves*, but unto us they did minister the things *which are now reported unto you* by them that have evangelized you."[11] Here the faith of the ancient Saints is described as employed, not merely on truths so far as mastered by the mind, but on truths beyond it, and even to the end withheld from its perfect apprehension.

[...]

4. This is a fit place to make some remarks on the Scripture sense of the word Mystery. It may seem a contradiction in terms to call Revelation a Mystery; but is not the book of the Revelation of St. John as great a mystery from beginning to end as the most abstruse doctrine the mind ever imagined? Yet it is even called a *Revelation*. How is this? The answer is simple. No revelation can be complete and systematic, from the weakness of the human intellect; *so far as* it is not such, it is mysterious. When nothing is revealed, nothing is known, and there is nothing to contemplate or marvel at; but when something is revealed, and only something, for all cannot be, there are forthwith difficulties and perplexities. A Revelation is religious doctrine viewed on its illuminated side; a Mystery is the selfsame doctrine viewed on the side unilluminated. Thus Religious Truth is neither light nor darkness, but both together; it is like the dim view of a country seen in the twilight, with forms half extricated from the darkness, with broken lines, and isolated masses. Revelation, in this way of considering it, is not a revealed *system*, but consists of a number

---

11. 1 Peter 1:10–12.

of detached and incomplete truths belonging to a vast system unrevealed, of doctrines and injunctions mysteriously connected together; that is, connected by unknown media, and bearing upon unknown portions of the system. And in this sense we see the propriety of calling St. John's prophecies, though highly mysterious, yet a revelation.

And such seems to be the meaning of the word Mystery in Scripture, a point which is sometimes disputed. Campbell, in his work on the Gospels, maintains that the word means a *secret*, and that, whatever be the subject of it in the New Testament, it is always, when mentioned, associated with the notion of its being now revealed. Thus, in his view, it is a word belonging solely to the Law, which was a system of types and shadows, and is utterly foreign to the Gospel, which has brought light instead of darkness. This sense might seem to be supported by our Lord's announcement (for instance) to His disciples, that to them was given to know the mysteries of His kingdom; and by His command to them at another time to speak abroad what they had heard from Him in secret. And St. Paul in like manner glories in the revelation of mysteries hid from the foundation of the world.

But the passages of Scripture admit, as I have suggested, of another interpretation. What was hidden altogether before Christ came, could not be a mystery; it became a Mystery, then for the first time, by being disclosed at His coming. What had never been dreamed of by "righteous men," before Him, when revealed, as *being* unexpected, if for no other reason, would be strange and startling. And such unquestionably is the meaning of St. Paul, when he uses the word; for he applies it, not to what was passed and over, but to what was the then state of the doctrine revealed. Thus in the text, 1 Corinthians 15:51–52, "Behold I show you a Mystery; we shall not all sleep, but we shall all be changed, in a moment, in the twinkling of an eye, at the last trump." The resurrection and consequent spiritualizing of the human body was not dreamed of by the philosophy of the world till Christ came, and, when revealed, was "mocked," as then first becoming a mystery. Reason is just where it was; and, as it could not discover it beforehand, so now it cannot account for it, or reconcile it to experience, or explain the manner of it: the utmost it does is by some faint analogies to show that it is not inconceivable. Again, St. Paul, speaking of marriage says, "This is a great Mystery, I mean, in its reference to Christ and the Church"; that is, the ordinance of marriage has an inward and spiritual meaning, contained in it and revealed through it, a certain bearing, undefined and therefore mysterious, toward the heavenly communion existing between Christ and the Church — as if for persons to place themselves in that human relation interested them in some secret way in the divine relation of which it is a figure. Again: "Great is the Mystery of piety; God was manifested in the flesh, justified in the Spirit, seen of Angels, preached unto the Gentiles, believed on in the world, received up into glory."[12] Now is the revelation of these truths a Manifestation (as above explained) or a Mystery? Surely the great secret has, by being revealed, only got so far as to be a Mystery, nothing more; nor could become a Manifestation (that is, a system comprehended as such by the human mind) without ceasing to be anything great at all. It must ever be small and superficial, viewed only as received by man; and is vast only when considered as that external truth into which each Christian may grow continually, and ever find fresh food for his soul.

As to the unknown, marvelous system of things spoken of in the text just quoted, it is described again, in an almost parallel passage, as regards the subject, though differently worded, in the Epistle to the Hebrews: "Ye are come unto Mount Zion, and unto the city of the living God, the heavenly Jerusalem, and to an innumerable company of Angels, to the full concourse and assembly

---

12. 1 Timothy 3:16.

of the first-born enrolled in heaven, and to God the Judge of all, and to the spirits of the perfected just, and to Jesus the Mediator of the New Covenant, and to the blood of sprinkling, that speaketh better things than that of Abel."[13] In like manner when St. Paul speaks of the election of the Gentiles as a Mystery revealed, the facts of the case show that it was still a mystery, and therefore but revealed to be a mystery, not a secret explained. We know that the Jews did stumble at it; why, if it was clear and obvious to reason? Certainly it was still a Mystery to them. Will it be objected that it had been plainly predicted? Surely not. The calling indeed of the Gentiles had been predicted, but not their equal participation with the Jews in all the treasures of the Covenant of grace, not the destruction of the Mosaic system. The prophets everywhere speak of the Jews as the head of the Gentiles; it was a new doctrine altogether (at least to the existing generation) that the election henceforth was to have no reference whatever to the Jews as a distinct people. This had hitherto been utterly hidden and unexpected; it emerged into a stumbling block, or Mystery, when the Gospel was preached, as on the other hand it became to all humble minds a marvel or mystery of mercy. Hence St. Paul speaks of the Mystery "which in other ages was not made known to the sons of men, that the Gentiles should be *fellow-heirs*, and of the *same body*, and *partakers of His promise in Christ* by the Gospel."[14]

5. [...] The practical inference to be drawn from this view is, first, that we should be very reverent in dealing with Revealed Truth; next, that we should avoid all rash theorizing and systematizing as relates to it, which is pretty much what looking into the Ark was under the Law: further, that we should be solicitous to hold it safely and entirely; moreover, that we should be zealous

---

13. Hebrews 12:22–24.
14. Ephesians 3:5.

and pertinacious in guarding it; and lastly, which is implied in all these, that we should religiously adhere to the form of words and the ordinances under which it comes to us, through which it is revealed to us, and apart from which the Revelation does not exist, there being nothing else given us by which to ascertain or enter into it.

The Tamworth
Reading Room

Part 6 (1841)

People say to me that it is but a dream to suppose that Christianity should regain the organic power in human society which once
it possessed. I cannot help that; I never said it could. I am not a
politician; I am proposing no measures, but exposing a fallacy,
and resisting a pretense. Let Benthamism[15] reign, if men have no

15. Newman is here referring to the late Enlightenment philosopher, Jeremy Bentham (1748-1832),
who is most famous for his moral and political theory of utilitarianism. Bentham argued that all
human conduct is driven by the pursuit of pleasure and the avoidance of pain. These two things,
Bentham argued, are the only sources for a truly rational moral and political system. The good life for
an individual, and the common good for a society, were determined, on the one hand, by

aspirations; but do not tell them to be romantic, and then solace them with glory; do not attempt by philosophy what once was done by religion. The ascendancy of Faith may be impracticable, but the reign of Knowledge is incomprehensible. The problem for statesmen of this age is how to educate the masses, and literature and science cannot give the solution.

Not so deems Sir Robert Peel; his firm belief and hope is, "that an increased sagacity will administer to an exalted faith; that it will make men not merely believe in the cold doctrines of Natural Religion, but that it will so prepare and temper the spirit and understanding, that they will be better qualified to comprehend the great scheme of human redemption." He certainly thinks that scientific pursuits have some considerable power of impressing religion upon the mind of the multitude. I think not, and will now say why.

Science gives us the grounds or premises from which religious truths are to be inferred; but it does not set about inferring them, much less does it reach the inference; that is not its province. It brings before us phenomena, and it leaves us, if we will, to call them works of design, wisdom, or benevolence; and further still, if we will, to proceed to confess an Intelligent Creator. We have to take its facts, and to give them a meaning, and to draw our own conclusions from them. First comes Knowledge, then a view, then reasoning, and then belief. This is why Science has so little of a religious tendency; deductions have no power of persuasion. The heart is commonly reached, not through the reason, but through the imagination, by means of direct impressions, by the testimony of facts and events, by history, by description. Per-

---

the maximization of pleasure for the maximum number of people, and on the other hand, by the minimization of pain and suffering. Bentham, like many other Enlightenment figures, saw religion as something merely subjective, personal, and irrational, though useful for the masses. Newman, of course, rejects this understanding of religion, and here critiques Bentham's utilitarianism for the way it reduces the desires of the human heart to the merely pleasurable and useful, whereas Christianity calls people to something greater beyond the lower goods of this world.

sons influence us, voices melt us, looks subdue us, deeds inflame us. Many a man will live and die upon a dogma: no man will be a martyr for a conclusion. A conclusion is but an opinion; it is not a thing which *is*, but which *we are* "*certain about*"; and it has often been observed, that we never say we are certain without implying that we doubt. To say that a thing *must* be is to admit that *it may not* be. No one, I say, will die for his own calculations; he dies for realities. This is why a literary religion is so little to be depended upon; it looks well in fair weather, but its doctrines are opinions, and, when called to suffer for them, it slips them between its folios or burns them at its hearth. And this again is the secret of the distrust and raillery with which moralists have been so commonly visited. They say and do not. Why? Because they are contemplating the fitness of things, and they live by the square, when they should be realizing their high maxims in the concrete. Now Sir Robert thinks better of natural history, chemistry, and astronomy, than of such ethics; but they too, what are they more than divinity *in posse*? He protests against "controversial divinity"; is *inferential* much better?

I have no confidence, then, in philosophers who cannot help being religious, and are Christians by implication. They sit at home and reach forward to distances which astonish us; but they hit without grasping and are sometimes as confident about shadows as about realities. They have worked out by a calculation the lie of a country which they never saw, and mapped it by means of a gazetteer; and like blind men, though they can put a stranger on his way, they cannot walk straight themselves, and do not feel it quite their business to walk at all.

Logic makes but a sorry rhetoric with the multitude; first shoot round corners, and you may not despair of converting by a syllogism. Tell men to gain notions of a Creator from His works, and, if they were to set about it (which nobody does), they would be jaded and wearied by the labyrinth they were tracing. Their minds would be gorged and surfeited by the logical operation. Logicians are more set upon concluding rightly, than on right conclusions. They cannot see the end for the process. Few men have that power of mind which may hold fast and firmly a variety of thoughts. We ridicule "men of one idea," but a great many of us are born to be such, and we should be happier if we knew it. To most men argument makes the point in hand only more doubtful, and considerably less impressive. After all, man is *not* a reasoning animal; he is a seeing, feeling, contemplating, acting animal. He is influenced by what is direct and precise. It is very well to freshen our impressions and convictions from physics, but to create them we must go elsewhere. Sir Robert Peel "never can think it possible that a mind can be so constituted, that, after being familiarized with the wonderful discoveries which have been made in every part of experimental science, it can retire from such contemplations without more enlarged conceptions of God's providence, and a higher reverence for His name." If he speaks of religious minds, he perpetrates a truism; if of irreligious, he insinuates a paradox.

Life is not long enough for a religion of inferences; we shall never have done beginning, if we determine to begin with proof. We shall ever be laying our foundations; we shall turn theology into evidences, and divines into textuaries. We shall never get at our first principles. Resolve to believe nothing, and you must prove your proofs and analyze your elements, sinking further and further, and finding "in the lowest depth a lower deep," till you come to the broad bosom of skepticism. I would rather be bound to defend the reasonableness of assuming that Christianity is true, than to demonstrate a moral governance from the physical world. Life is for action. If we insist on proofs for everything, we shall never come to action: to act you must assume, and that assumption is faith.

Let no one suppose that in saying this I am maintaining that

all proofs are equally difficult, and all propositions equally debat-
able. Some assumptions are greater than others, and some doctrines involve postulates larger than others, and more numerous.
I only say that impressions lead to action, and that reasonings
lead from it. Knowledge of premises, and inferences upon them
— this is not to *live*. It is very well as a matter of liberal curiosity and of philosophy to analyze our modes of thought; but let
this come second, and when there is leisure for it, and then our
examinations will in many ways even be subservient to action.
But if we commence with scientific knowledge and argumenta-
tive proof, or lay any great stress upon it as the basis of personal
Christianity, or attempt to make man moral and religious by Libraries and Museums, let us in consistency take chemists for our
cooks, and mineralogists for our masons.

Now I wish to state all this as matter of fact, to be judged by
the candid testimony of any persons whatever. Why we are so
constituted that Faith, not Knowledge or Argument, is our principle of action, is a question with which I have nothing to do; but
I think it is a fact, and if it be such, we must resign ourselves to it
as best we may, unless we take refuge in the intolerable paradox,
that the mass of men are created for nothing, and are meant to
leave life as they entered it. So well has this practically been understood in all ages of the world, that no Religion has yet been
a Religion of physics or of philosophy. It has ever been synony-
mous with Revelation. It never has been a deduction from what
we know: it has ever been an assertion of what we are to believe.
It has never lived in a conclusion; it has ever been a message,
or a history, or a vision. No legislator or priest ever dreamed of
educating our moral nature by science or by argument. There is
no difference here between true Religions and pretended. Moses
was instructed, not to reason from the creation, but to work mir-
acles. Christianity is a history supernatural, and almost scenic:
It tells us what its Author is, by telling us what He has done. I

have no wish at all to speak otherwise than respectfully of con-
scientious Dissenters, but I have heard it said by those who were
not their enemies, and who had known much of their preaching,
that they had often heard narrow-minded and bigoted clergy-
men, and often Dissenting ministers of a far more intellectual
cast; but that Dissenting teaching came to nothing — that it was
dissipated in thoughts which had no point, and inquiries which
converged to no center, that it ended as it began, and sent away
its hearers as it found them — whereas the instruction in the
Church, with all its defects and mistakes, comes to some end, for
it started from some beginning. Such is the difference between
the dogmatism of faith and the speculations of logic.

Lord Brougham himself, as we have already seen, has recognized the force of this principle. He has not left his philosophical
religion to argument; he has committed it to the keeping of the
imagination. Why should he depict a great republic of letters,
and an intellectual Pantheon, but that he feels that instances and
patterns, not logical reasonings, are the living conclusions which
alone have a hold over the affections, or can form the character?

A Letter to the Duke of Norfolk

Part 5, "On Conscience" (excerpt) (1875)

It seems, then, that there are extreme cases in which Conscience may come into collision with the word of a Pope, and is to be followed in spite of that word. Now I wish to place this proposition on a broader basis, acknowledged by all Catholics, and, in order to do this satisfactorily, as I began with the prophecies of Scripture and the primitive Church, when I spoke of the Pope's prerogatives, so now I must begin with the Creator and His creature, when I would draw out the prerogatives and the supreme authority of Conscience.

I say, then, that the Supreme Being is of a certain character, which, expressed in human language, we call ethical. He has the attributes of justice, truth, wisdom, sanctity, benevolence, and mercy, as eternal characteristics in His nature, the very Law of His being, identical with Himself; and next, when He became Creator, He implanted this Law, which is Himself, in the intelligence of all His rational creatures. The Divine Law, then, is the rule of ethical truth, the standard of right and wrong, a sovereign, irreversible, absolute authority in the presence of men and Angels. "The eternal law," says St. Augustine, "is the Divine Reason or Will of God, commanding the observance, forbidding the disturbance, of the natural order of things." "The natural law," says St. Thomas, "is an impression of the Divine Light in us, a participation of the eternal law in the rational creature" (Gousset, *Theol. Moral.*, t. i. pp. 24, etc.). This law, as apprehended in the minds of individual men, is called "conscience"; and though it may suffer refraction in passing into the intellectual medium of each, it is not therefore so affected as to lose its character of being the Divine Law, but still has, as such, the prerogative of commanding obedience. "The Divine Law," says Cardinal Gousset, "is the supreme rule of actions; our thoughts, desires, words, acts, all that man is, is subject to the domain of the law of God; and this law is the rule of our conduct by means of our conscience. Hence it is never lawful to go against our conscience; as the fourth Lateran Council says, '*Quidquid fit contra conscientiam, ædificat ad gehennam.*'"[16]

This view of conscience, I know, is very different from that ordinarily taken of it, both by the science and literature, and by the public opinion, of this day. It is founded on the doctrine that conscience is the voice of God, whereas it is fashionable on all hands now to consider it in one way or another a creation

---

16. "Whatever is done against conscience, builds up towards Gehenna."

of man. Of course, there are great and broad exceptions to this statement. It is not true of many or most religious bodies of men; especially not of their teachers and ministers. When Anglicans, Wesleyans, the various Presbyterian sects in Scotland, and other denominations among us, speak of conscience, they mean what we mean, the voice of God in the nature and heart of man, as distinct from the voice of Revelation. They speak of a principle planted within us, before we have had any training, although training and experience are necessary for its strength, growth, and due formation. They consider it a constituent element of the mind, as our perception of other ideas may be, as our powers of reasoning, as our sense of order and the beautiful, and our other intellectual endowments. They consider it, as Catholics consider it, to be the internal witness of both the existence and the law of God. They think it holds of God, and not of man, as an Angel walking on the earth would be no citizen or dependent of the Civil Power. They would not allow, any more than we do, that it could be resolved into any combination of principles in our nature, more elementary than itself; nay, though it may be called, and is, a law of the mind, they would not grant that it was nothing more; I mean, that it was not a dictate, nor conveyed the notion of responsibility, of duty, of a threat and a promise, with a vividness which discriminated it from all other constituents of our nature.

This, at least, is how I read the doctrine of Protestants as well as of Catholics. The rule and measure of duty is not utility, nor expedience, nor the happiness of the greatest number, nor State convenience, nor fitness, order, and the *pulchrum*.[17] Conscience is not a long-sighted selfishness, nor a desire to be consistent with oneself; but it is a messenger from Him, who, both in nature and in grace, speaks to us behind a veil, and teaches and rules us by

---

17. "Beautiful."

His representatives. Conscience is the aboriginal Vicar of Christ, a prophet in its informations, a monarch in its peremptoriness, a priest in its blessings and anathemas, and, even though the eternal priesthood throughout the Church could cease to be, in it the sacerdotal principle would remain and would have a sway.

Words such as these are idle empty verbiage to the great world of philosophy now. All through my day there has been a resolute warfare, I had almost said conspiracy against the rights of conscience, as I have described it. Literature and science have been embodied in great institutions in order to put it down. Noble buildings have been reared as fortresses against that spiritual, invisible influence which is too subtle for science and too profound for literature. Chairs in Universities have been made the seats of an antagonist tradition. Public writers, day after day, have indoctrinated the minds of innumerable readers with theories subversive of its claims. As in Roman times, and in the middle age, its supremacy was assailed by the arm of physical force, so now the intellect is put in operation to sap the foundations of a power which the sword could not destroy. We are told that conscience is but a twist in primitive and untutored man; that its dictate is an imagination; that the very notion of guiltiness, which that dictate enforces, is simply irrational, for how can there possibly be freedom of will, how can there be consequent responsibility, in that infinite eternal network of cause and effect, in which we helplessly lie? And what retribution have we to fear, when we have had no real choice to do good or evil?

[...] Conscience has rights because it has duties; but in this age, with a large portion of the public, it is the very right and freedom of conscience to dispense with conscience, to ignore a Lawgiver and Judge, to be independent of unseen obligations. It becomes a license to take up any or no religion, to take up this or that and let it go again, to go to church, to go to chapel, to boast of being above all religions and to be an impartial critic of each of them. Conscience is a stern monitor, but in this century it has been superseded by a counterfeit, which the eighteen centuries prior to it never heard of, and could not have mistaken for it, if they had. It is the right of self-will.

[...]

So indeed it is; did the Pope speak against Conscience in the true sense of the word, he would commit a suicidal act. He would be cutting the ground from under his feet. His very mission is to proclaim the moral law, and to protect and strengthen that "Light which enlighteneth every man that cometh into the world."[18] On the law of conscience and its sacredness are founded both his authority in theory and his power in fact. Whether this or that particular Pope in this bad world always kept this great truth in view in all he did, it is for history to tell. I am considering here the Papacy in its office and its duties, and in reference to those who acknowledge its claims. They are not bound by the Pope's personal character or private acts, but by his formal teaching. Thus viewing his position, we shall find that it is by the universal sense of right and wrong, the consciousness of transgression, the pangs of guilt, and the dread of retribution, as first principles deeply lodged in the hearts of men, it is thus and only thus, that he has gained his footing in the world and achieved his success. It is his claim to come from the Divine Lawgiver, in order to elicit, protect, and enforce those truths which the Lawgiver has sown in our very nature, it is this and this only that is the explanation of his length of life more than antediluvian. The championship of the Moral Law and of conscience is his *raison d'être*. The fact of his mission is the answer to the complaints of those who feel the insufficiency of the natural light; and the insufficiency of that light is the justification of his mission.

[...]

---

18. John 1:9

1. First, I am using the word "conscience" in the high sense in which I have already explained it — not as a fancy or an opinion, but as a dutiful obedience to what claims to be a divine voice, speaking within us; and that this is the view properly to be taken of it, I shall not attempt to prove here, but shall assume it as a first principle.

2. Secondly, I observe that conscience is not a judgment upon any speculative truth, any abstract doctrine, but bears immediately on conduct, on something to be done or not done. "Conscience," says St. Thomas, "is the practical judgment or dictate of reason, by which we judge what *hic et nunc*[19] is to be done as being good, or to be avoided as evil." Hence conscience cannot come into direct collision with the Church's or the Pope's infallibility; which is engaged in general propositions, and in the condemnation of particular and given errors.

3. Next, I observe that, conscience being a practical dictate, a collision is possible between it and the Pope's authority only when the Pope legislates, or gives particular orders, and the like. But a Pope is not infallible in his laws, nor in his commands, nor in his acts of state, nor in his administration, nor in his public policy. Let it be observed that the Vatican Council has left him just as it found him here. Mr. Gladstone's language on this point is to me quite unintelligible. [...] What have excommunication and interdict to do with Infallibility? Was St. Peter infallible on that occasion at Antioch when St. Paul withstood him? Was St. Victor infallible when he separated from his communion the Asiatic Churches? Or Liberius when in like manner he excommunicated Athanasius? And, to come to later times, was Gregory XIII, when he had a medal struck in honor of the Bartholomew massacre? Or Paul IV in his conduct towards Elizabeth? Or Sixtus V when he blessed the Armada? Or Urban VIII when he

---

19. "Here and now."

persecuted Galileo? No Catholic ever pretends that these Popes were infallible in these acts. Since then infallibility alone could block the exercise of conscience, and the Pope is not infallible in that subject-matter in which conscience is of supreme authority, no deadlock, such as is implied in the objection which I am answering, can take place between conscience and the Pope.

4. But, of course, I have to say again, lest I should be misunderstood, that when I speak of Conscience, I mean conscience truly so called. When it has the right of opposing the supreme, though not infallible Authority of the Pope, it must be something more than that miserable counterfeit which, as I have said above, now goes by the name. If in a particular case it is to be taken as a sacred and sovereign monitor, its dictate, in order to prevail against the voice of the Pope, must follow upon serious thought, prayer, and all available means of arriving at a right judgment on the matter in question. And further, obedience to the Pope is what is called "in possession"; that is, the *onus probandi*[20] of establishing a case against him lies, as in all cases of exception, on the side of conscience. Unless a man is able to say to himself, as in the Presence of God, that he must not, and dare not, act upon the Papal injunction, he is bound to obey it, and would commit a great sin in disobeying it. *Prima facie* it is his bounden duty, even from a sentiment of loyalty, to believe the Pope right and to act accordingly. He must vanquish that mean, ungenerous, selfish, vulgar spirit of his nature, which, at the very first rumor of a command, places itself in opposition to the Superior who gives it, asks itself whether he is not exceeding his right, and rejoices, in a moral and practical matter to commence with skepticism. He must have no willful determination to exercise a right of thinking, saying, doing just what he pleases, the question of truth and falsehood, right and wrong, the duty if possible of obedience, the

---

20. "Burden of proof."

love of speaking as his Head speaks, and of standing in all cases on his Head's side, being simply discarded. If this necessary rule were observed, collisions between the Pope's authority and the authority of conscience would be very rare. On the other hand, in the fact that, after all, in extraordinary cases, the conscience of each individual is free, we have a safeguard and security, were security necessary (which is a most gratuitous supposition), that no Pope ever will be able, as the objection supposes, to create a false conscience for his own ends.

[...]

Thus, if the Pope told the English Bishops to order their priests to stir themselves energetically in favor of teetotalism, and a particular priest was fully persuaded that abstinence from wine, etc., was practically a Gnostic error, and therefore felt he could not so exert himself without sin; or suppose there was a Papal order to hold lotteries in each mission for some religious object, and a priest could say in God's sight that he believed lotteries to be morally wrong, that priest in either of these cases would commit a sin *hic et nunc* if he obeyed the Pope, whether he was right or wrong in his opinion, and, if wrong, although he had not taken proper pains to get at the truth of the matter.

[...]

I add one remark. Certainly, if I am obliged to bring religion into after-dinner toasts (which indeed does not seem quite the thing), I shall drink — to the Pope, if you please — still, to Conscience first, and to the Pope afterward.

Biglietto Speech

Delivered May 12, 1879, upon receiving official
notification of his being made a cardinal

*Vi ringrazio, Monsignore, per la participazione che m'avete fatto
dell' alto onore che il Santo Padre si è degnato conferire sulla mia
umile persona —* [21]

And, if I ask your permission to continue my address to
you, not in your musical language, but in my own dear mother
tongue, it is because in the latter I can better express my feelings
on this most gracious announcement which you have brought to
me than if I attempted what is above me.

First of all then, I am led to speak of the wonder and pro-

---

21. "I thank you, Monsignor, for your participation in the high honor that the Holy Father has deigned
to confer on my humble person."

found gratitude which came upon me, and which is upon me still, at the condescension and love toward me of the Holy Father in singling me out for so immense an honor. It was a great surprise. Such an elevation had never come into my thoughts and seemed to be out of keeping with all my antecedents. I had passed through many trials, but they were over; and now the end of all things had almost come to me, and I was at peace. And was it possible that after all I had lived through so many years for this?

Nor is it easy to see how I could have borne so great a shock, had not the Holy Father resolved on a second act of condescension toward me, which tempered it, and was to all who heard of it a touching evidence of his kindly and generous nature. He felt for me, and he told me the reasons why he raised me to this high position. Besides other words of encouragement, he said his act was a recognition of my zeal and good service for so many years in the Catholic cause; moreover, he judged it would give pleasure to English Catholics, and even to Protestant England, if I received some mark of his favor. After such gracious words from his Holiness, I should have been insensible and heartless if I had had scruples any longer.

This is what he had the kindness to say to me, and what could I want more? In a long course of years I have made many mistakes. I have nothing of that high perfection which belongs to the writings of Saints, *viz.*, that error cannot be found in them; but what I trust that I may claim all through what I have written, is this: an honest intention, an absence of private ends, a temper of obedience, a willingness to be corrected, a dread of error, a desire to serve Holy Church, and, through Divine mercy, a fair measure of success. And, I rejoice to say, to one great mischief I have from the first opposed myself. For thirty, forty, fifty years I have resisted to the best of my powers the spirit of liberalism in religion. Never did Holy Church need champions against it more sorely than now, when, alas! it is an error overspreading, as a snare, the whole earth; and on this great occasion, when it is natural for one who is in my place to look out upon the world, and upon Holy Church as in it, and upon her future, it will not, I hope, be considered out of place, if I renew the protest against it which I have made so often.

Liberalism in religion is the doctrine that there is no positive truth in religion, but that one creed is as good as another, and this is the teaching which is gaining substance and force daily. It is inconsistent with any recognition of any religion, as *true*. It teaches that all are to be tolerated, for all are matters of opinion. Revealed religion is not a truth, but a sentiment and a taste; not an objective fact, not miraculous; and it is the right of each individual to make it say just what strikes his fancy. Devotion is not necessarily founded on faith. Men may go to Protestant Churches and to Catholic, may get good from both and belong to neither. They may fraternize together in spiritual thoughts and feelings, without having any views at all of doctrine in common, or seeing the need of them. Since, then, religion is so personal a peculiarity and so private a possession, we must of necessity ignore it in the intercourse of man with man. If a man puts on a new religion every morning, what is that to you? It is as impertinent to think about a man's religion as about his sources of income or his management of his family. Religion is in no sense the bond of society.

Hitherto the civil Power has been Christian. Even in countries separated from the Church, as in my own, the *dictum* was in force, when I was young, that: "Christianity was the law of the land." Now, everywhere that goodly framework of society, which is the creation of Christianity, is throwing off Christianity. The *dictum* to which I have referred, with a hundred others which followed upon it, is gone, or is going everywhere; and, by the end of the century, unless the Almighty interferes, it will be *forgotten*. Hitherto, it has been considered that religion alone, with its supernatural sanctions, was strong enough to secure submission of the masses of our population to law and order; now the Philosophers and Politicians are bent on satisfying this problem without the aid of Christianity. Instead of the Church's authority and teaching, they would substitute first of all a universal and a thoroughly secular education, calculated to bring home to every individual that to be orderly, industrious, and sober, is his personal interest. Then, for great working principles to take the place of religion, for the use of the masses thus carefully educated, it provides — the broad fundamental ethical truths, of justice, benevolence, veracity, and the like; proved experience; and those natural laws which exist and act spontaneously in society, and in social matters, whether physical or psychological; for instance, in government, trade, finance, sanitary experiments, and the intercourse of nations. As to Religion, it is a private luxury, which a man may have if he will; but which of course he must pay for, and which he must not obtrude upon others, or indulge in to their annoyance.

The general character of this great *apostasia* is one and the same everywhere; but in detail, and in character, it varies in different countries. For myself, I would rather speak of it in my own country, which I know. There, I think it threatens to have a formidable success; though it is not easy to see what will be its ultimate issue. At first sight it might be thought that Englishmen are too religious for a movement which, on the Continent, seems to be founded on infidelity; but the misfortune with us is, that, though it ends in infidelity as in other places, it does not necessarily arise out of infidelity. It must be recollected that the religious sects, which sprang up in England three centuries ago, and which are so powerful now, have ever been fiercely opposed to the Union of Church and State, and would advocate the un-Christianizing of the monarchy and all that belongs to it, under the notion that such a catastrophe would make Christianity much more pure and much more powerful. Next the liberal principle is forced on us from the necessity of the case. Consider what follows from the very fact of these many sects. They constitute the religion, it is supposed, of half the population; and, recollect, our mode of government is popular. Every dozen men taken at random whom you meet in the streets has a share in political power — when you inquire into their forms of belief, perhaps they represent one or other of as many as seven religions; how can they possibly act together in municipal or in national matters, if each insists on the recognition of his own religious denomination? All action would be at a deadlock unless the subject of religion was ignored. We cannot help ourselves. And, thirdly, it must be borne in mind, that there is much in the liberalistic theory which is good and true; for example, not to say more, the precepts of justice, truthfulness, sobriety, self-command, benevolence, which, as I have already noted, are among its avowed principles, and the natural laws of society. It is not till we find that this array of principles is intended to supersede, to block out, religion, that we pronounce it to be evil. There never was a device of the Enemy so cleverly framed and with such promise of success. And already it has answered to the expectations which have been formed of it. It is sweeping into its own ranks great numbers of able, earnest, virtuous men, elderly men of approved antecedents, young men with a career before them.

Such is the state of things in England, and it is well that it should be realized by all of us; but it must not be supposed for a moment that I am afraid of it. I lament it deeply, because I foresee that it may be the ruin of many souls; but I have no fear at all that it really can do aught of serious harm to the Word of God, to Holy Church, to our Almighty King, the Lion of the tribe of Judah, Faithful and True, or to His Vicar on earth. Christianity has been too often in what seemed deadly peril, that we should fear for it any new trial now. So far is certain; on the other hand, what is uncertain, and in these great contests commonly is uncertain, and what is commonly a great surprise, when it is witnessed, is the particular mode by which, in the event, Providence rescues and saves His elect inheritance. Sometimes our enemy is turned into a friend; sometimes he is despoiled of that special virulence of evil which was so threatening; sometimes he falls to pieces of himself; sometimes he does just so much as is beneficial, and then is removed. Commonly the Church has nothing more to do than to go on in her own proper duties, in confidence and peace; to stand still and to see the salvation of God.

> *Mansueti hereditabunt terram,*
> *Et delectabuntur in multitudine pacis.*[22]

---

22. "But the meek shall possess the land, and delight themselves in abundant prosperity" (Ps 37:11, RSV).

Sermons

The Danger of Accomplishments

In *Parochial and Plain Sermons,* Volume II (1831)

"In the hearts of all that are wise hearted, I have put wisdom."
Exodus 31:6

St. Luke differed from his fellow-evangelists and fellow-disciples in having received the advantages of (what is called) a liberal education. In this respect he resembled St. Paul, who, with equal accomplishments appears to have possessed even more learning. He is said to have been a native of Antioch, a city celebrated for the refined habits and cultivated intellect of its inhabitants; and his profession was that of a physician or surgeon, which of itself evidences him to have been in point of education something above the generality of men. This is confirmed by the character of his writings, which are superior in composition to any part of the New Testament, excepting some of St. Paul's Epistles.

There are persons who doubt whether what are called "accomplishments," whether in literature or in the fine arts, can be consistent with deep and practical seriousness of mind. They think that attention to these argues a lightness of mind, and, at least, takes up time which might be better employed; and, I confess, at first sight they seem to be able to say much in defense of their opinion. Yet, notwithstanding, St. Luke and St. Paul were accomplished men, and evidently took pleasure in their accomplishments.

I am not speaking of human *learning*; this also many men think inconsistent with simple uncorrupted faith. They suppose that learning must make a man proud. This is of course a great mistake; but of it I am not speaking, but of an over-jealousy of *accomplishments*, the elegant arts and studies, such as poetry, literary composition, painting, music, and the like; which are considered (not indeed to make a man *proud*, but) to make him *trifling*. Of this opinion, how far it is true, and how far not true, I am going to speak: being led to the consideration of it by the known fact, that St. Luke was a polished writer, and yet an Evangelist.

Now, that the accomplishments I speak of have a *tendency* to make us trifling and unmanly, and therefore are to be viewed by each of us with suspicion as far as regards himself, I am ready to admit, and shall presently make clear. I allow, that in matter of fact, refinement and luxury, elegance and effeminacy, go together. Antioch, the most polished, was the most voluptuous city of Asia. But the *abuse* of good things is no argument against the things themselves; mental cultivation *may* be a divine gift, though it is abused. All God's gifts are perverted by man; health, strength, intellectual power, are all turned by sinners to bad purposes, yet they are not evil in themselves: therefore an acquaintance with the elegant arts may be a gift and a good, and intended to be an instrument of God's glory, though numbers who have it are rendered thereby indolent, luxurious, and feeble-minded.

But the account of the building of the Tabernacle in the wilderness, from which the text is taken, is decisive on this point. It is too long to read to you, but a few verses will remind you of the nature of it. "Thou shalt speak unto all that are wise hearted, whom I have filled with the spirit of wisdom, that they may make Aaron's garments to consecrate him, that he may minister unto me in the priest's office." "See I have called by name Bezaleel … and have filled him with the Spirit of God, in wisdom and in understanding, and in knowledge, and in all manner of workmanship, to devise cunning works, to work in gold, and in silver, and in brass, and in cutting of stones, to set them, and in carving of timber, to work all manner of workmanship." "Take ye from among you an offering unto the Lord; whosoever is of a willing heart let him bring it, an offering of the Lord, gold, and silver, and brass, and blue, and purple, and scarlet and fine linen, and goats' hair, and rams' skins dyed red, and badgers' skins, and shittim wood, and oil for the light, and spices for anointing oil, and for the sweet incense, and onyx stones, and stones to be set for the ephod, and for the breast-plate. And every wise hearted among you shall come and make all that the Lord hath commanded."[23]

How then is it, that what in itself is of so excellent, and (I may say) divine in nature, is yet so commonly perverted? I proceed to state what is the danger, as it appears to me, of being accomplished, with a view to answer this question.

---

23. Exodus 27:3; 31:2–5; 35:5–10.

Now the *danger* of an elegant and polite education is that it separates feeling and acting; it teaches us to think, speak, and be affected aright, without forcing us to practice what is right. I will take an illustration of this, though somewhat a familiar one, from the effect produced upon the mind by reading what is commonly called a romance or novel, which comes under the description of polite literature, of which I am speaking. Such works contain many good sentiments (I am taking the better sort of them); characters too are introduced, virtuous, noble, patient under suffering, and triumphing at length over misfortune. The great truths of religion are upheld, we will suppose, and enforced; and our affections excited and interested in what is good and true. But it is all fiction; it does not exist out of a book which contains the beginning and end of it. *We* have nothing *to do*; we read, are affected, softened, or roused, and that is all; we cool again — nothing comes of it. Now observe the effect of this. God has made us feel in order that we may *go on to act* in consequence of feeling; if then we allow our feelings to be excited without acting upon them, we do mischief to the moral system within us, just as we might spoil a watch, or other piece of mechanism, by playing with the wheels of it. We weaken its springs, and they cease to act truly. Accordingly, when we have got into the habit of amusing ourselves with these works of fiction, we come at length to feel the excitement without the slightest thought or tendency to act upon it; and, since it is very difficult to begin any duty *without* some emotion or other (that is, to begin on mere principles of dry reasoning), a grave question arises, how, after destroying the connection between feeling and acting, how shall we get ourselves to act when circumstances make it our duty to do so? For instance, we will say we have read again and again of the heroism of facing danger, and we have glowed with the thought of its nobleness. We have felt how great it is to bear pain, and submit to indignities, rather than wound our conscience; and all this, again and again, when we had no opportunity of carrying our good feelings into practice. Now, suppose at length we actually come into trial, and let us say, our feelings become roused, as often before, at the thought of boldly resisting temptations to cowardice, shall we therefore do our duty, quitting ourselves like men? Rather, we are likely to talk loudly, and then run from the danger. Why? Rather let us ask, why *not*? What is to keep us from yielding? Because we *feel* aright? Nay, we have again and again felt aright, and thought aright, without accustoming ourselves to act aright, and, though there was an original connection in our minds between feeling and acting, there is none now; the wires within us, as they may be called, are loosened and powerless.

And what is here instanced of fortitude, is true in all cases of duty. The refinement which literature gives is that of thinking, feeling, knowing and speaking, right, not of acting right; and thus, while it makes the manners amiable, and the conversation decorous and agreeable, it has no tendency to make the conduct, the practice of the man, *virtuous*.

Observe, I have supposed the works of fiction I speak of to inculcate right sentiments; though such works (playbooks for example) are often vicious and immoral. But even at best, supposing them well principled, still after all, at best, they are, I say, dangerous, in themselves; that is, if we allow refinement to stand in the place of hardy, rough-handed obedience. It follows, that I am much opposed to certain *religious* novels, which some persons think so useful: that they sometimes do good, I am far from denying; but they do more harm than good. They do harm on the whole; they lead men to cultivate the religious affections separate from religious practice. And here I might speak of that entire religious system (miscalled religious) which makes Christian faith consist, not in the honest and plain practice of what is right, but in the luxury of excited religious feeling, in a mere meditating on our Blessed Lord, and dwelling as in a reverie on what He has done for us; for such indolent contemplation will no more sanctify a man *in fact* than reading a poem or listening to a chant or psalm-tune.

The case is the same with the arts last alluded to, poetry and music. These are especially likely to make us unmanly, if we are not on our guard, as exciting emotions without ensuring correspondent practice, and so destroying the connection between feeling and acting; for I here mean by unmanliness the inability to do with ourselves what we wish — the saying fine things and yet lying slothfully on our couch, as if we could not get up, though we ever so much wished it.

And here I must notice something besides in elegant accomplishments, which goes to make us over-refined and fastidious, and falsely delicate. In books, everything is made beautiful in its way. Pictures are drawn of *complete* virtue; little is said about failures, and little or nothing of the drudgery of ordinary, everyday obedience, which is neither poetical nor interesting. True faith teaches us to do numberless disagreeable things for Christ's sake, to bear petty annoyances, which we find written down in no book. In most books Christian conduct is made grand, elevated, and splendid; so that any one, who only knows of true religion from books, and not from actual endeavors to be religious, is sure to be offended at religion when he actually comes upon it, from the roughness and humbleness of his duties, and his necessary deficiencies in doing them. It is beautiful in a picture to wash the disciples' feet; but the sands of the real desert have no luster in them to compensate for the servile nature of the occupation.

And further still, it must be observed, that the art of composing, which is a chief accomplishment, has in itself a tendency to make us artificial and insincere. For to be ever attending to the fitness and propriety of our words, is (or at least there is the risk of its being) a kind of acting; and knowing what can be said on both sides of a subject is a main step toward thinking the one side as good as the other. Hence men in ancient times, who cultivated polite literature, went by the name of "Sophists"; that is, men who wrote elegantly, and talked eloquently, on any subject whatever, right or wrong. St. Luke perchance might have been such a Sophist, had he not been a Christian.

Such are some of the dangers of elegant accomplishments; and they beset more or less all educated persons; and of these perhaps not the least such females as happen to have no very direct duties, and are above the drudgery of common life, and hence are apt to become fastidious and fine — to love a luxurious ease, and to amuse themselves in mere elegant pursuits, the while they admire and profess what is religious and virtuous, and think that they really possess the character of mind which they esteem.

With these thoughts before us, it is necessary to look back to the Scripture instances which I began by adducing, to avoid the conclusion that accomplishments are positively dangerous, and unworthy a Christian. But St. Luke and St. Paul show us, that we may be sturdy workers in the Lord's service, and bear our cross manfully, though we be adorned with all the learning of the Egyptians; or rather, that the resources of literature, and the graces of a cultivated mind, may be made both a lawful source of enjoyment to the possessor, and a means of introducing and recommending the Truth to others; while the history of the Tabernacle shows that all the cunning arts and precious possessions of this world may be consecrated to a religious service, and be made to speak of the world to come.

I conclude then with the following cautions, to which the foregoing remarks lead. First, we must avoid giving too much time to lighter occupations; and next, we must never allow ourselves to read works of fiction or poetry, or to interest ourselves in the fine arts for the mere sake of the things themselves: but keep in mind all along that we are Christians and accountable beings, who have fixed principles of right and wrong, by which all things must be tried, and have religious habits to be matured within them, toward which all things are to be made subservient. Nothing is more common among accomplished people than the habit of reading books so entirely for reading's sake, as to praise and blame the actions and persons described in a random way, according to their fancy, not considering whether they are really good or bad according to the standard of moral truth. I would not be austere; but when this is done habitually, surely it is dangerous. Such too is the abuse of poetical talent, that sacred gift. Nothing is more common than to fall into the practice of uttering fine sentiments, particularly in letter writing, as a matter of course, or a kind of elegant display. Nothing more common in singing than to use words which have a light meaning, or a bad one. All these things are hurtful to seriousness of character. It is for this reason (to put aside others) that the profession of stage-players, and again of orators, is a dangerous one. They learn to say good things, and to excite in themselves vehement feelings, about nothing at all.

If we are in earnest, we shall let nothing lightly pass by which may do us good, nor shall we dare to trifle with such sacred subjects as morality and religious duty. We shall apply all we read to ourselves; and this almost without intending to do so, from the mere sincerity and honesty of our desire to please God. We shall be suspicious of all such good thoughts and wishes, and we shall shrink from all such exhibitions of our principles, as fall short of action. We shall aim at doing right, and so glorifying our Father, and shall exhort and constrain others to do so also; but as for talking on the appropriate subjects of religious meditation, and *trying* to show piety, and to excite corresponding feelings in another, even though our nearest friend, far from doing this, we shall account it a snare and a mischief. Yet this is what many persons consider the highest part of religion, and call it spiritual conversation, the test of a spiritual mind; whereas, putting aside the incipient and occasional hypocrisy, and again the immodesty of it, I call all formal and intentional expression of religions emotions, all studied passionate discourse, *dissipation* — dissipation the same in nature, though different in subject, as what is commonly so called; for it is a drain and a waste of our religious and moral strength, a general weakening of our spiritual powers (as I have already shown); and all for what? For the pleasure of the immediate excitement. Who can deny that this religious disorder is a parallel case to that of the sensualist? Nay, precisely the same as theirs, from whom the religionists in question think themselves very far removed, of the fashionable world I mean, who read works of fiction, frequent the public shows, are ever on the watch for novelties, and affect a pride of manners and a "mincing"[24] deportment, and are ready with all kinds of good thoughts and keen emotions on all occasions.

Of all such as abuse the decencies and elegancies of moral truth into a means of luxurious enjoyment, what would a prophet of God say? Hear the words of the holy Ezekiel, that stern rough man of God, a true Saint in the midst of a self-indulgent, high-professing people: "Thou son of man, the children of thy people still are talking against thee by the walls and in the doors of the houses, and speak one to another, every one to his brother, saying, Come, I pray you, and hear what is the word that cometh forth from the Lord. And they come unto thee as the people cometh, and they sit before thee as My people, and they hear thy words, but they will not do them: for with their mouth they show much love, but their heart goeth after their covetousness. And, lo, thou art unto them as a very lovely song of one that hath a pleasant voice, and can play well on an instrument: for they hear

---

24. Isaiah 3:16.

thy words, but they do them not."[25]

Or, consider St. Paul's words, which are still more impressive, because he was himself a man of learning and accomplishments, and took pleasure, in due place, in the pursuits to which these give rise:

"Preach the word; be instant in season, out of season; reprove, rebuke, exhort, with all long-suffering and doctrine. For the time will come when they will not endure sound doctrine; but after their own lusts shall they heap to themselves teachers, having itching ears. And they shall turn away their ears from the Truth, and shall be turned unto fables." "Watch ye, stand fast in the faith, quit you like men, be strong."[26]

25. Ezekial 33:30–32.
26. 2 Timothy 4:2–4; 1 Corinthians 16:13.

Mental Sufferings of Our Lord in His Passion

In *Discourses Addressed to Mixed Congregations* (1848)

Every passage in the history of our Lord and Savior is of unfathomable depth and affords inexhaustible matter of contemplation. All that concerns Him is infinite, and what we first discern is but the surface of that which begins and ends in eternity. It would be presumptuous for anyone short of saints and doctors to attempt to comment on His words and deeds, except in the way of meditation; but meditation and mental prayer are so much a duty in all who wish to cherish true faith and love toward Him, that it may be allowed us, my brethren, under the guidance of holy men who have gone before us, to dwell and enlarge upon what otherwise would more fitly be adored than scrutinized. And certain times of the year, this especially, call upon us to consider, as closely and minutely as we can, even the more sacred portions of the Gospel history. I would rather be thought feeble or officious in my treatment of them, than wanting to the Season; and so I now proceed because the religious usage of the Church requires it, and though any individual preacher may well shrink from it, to direct your thoughts to a subject, especially suitable now, and about which many of us perhaps think very little, the sufferings which our Lord endured in His innocent and sinless soul.

You know, my brethren, that our Lord and Savior, though He was God, was also perfect man; and hence He had not only a body, but a soul likewise, such as ours, though pure from all stain of evil. He did not take a body without a soul, God forbid! for that would not have been to become man. How would He have sanctified our nature by taking a nature which was not ours? Man without a soul is on a level with the beasts of the field; but our Lord came to save a race capable of praising and obeying Him, possessed of immortality, though that immortality had lost its promised blessedness. Man was created in the image of God, and that image is in his soul; when then his Maker, by an unspeakable condescension, came in his nature, He took on Himself a soul in order to take on Him a body; He took on Him a soul as the means of His union with a body; He took on Him in the first place the soul, then the body of man, both at once, but in this order, the soul and the body; He Himself created the soul which He took on Himself, while He took His body from the flesh of the Blessed Virgin, His Mother. Thus He became perfect man with body and soul; and as He took on Him a body of flesh and nerves, which admitted of wounds and death, and was capable of suffering, so did He take a soul, too, which was susceptible of that suffering, and moreover was susceptible of the pain and sorrow which are proper to a human soul; and, as His atoning passion was undergone in the body, so it was undergone in the soul also.

As the solemn days proceed, we shall be especially called on, my brethren, to consider His sufferings in the body, His seizure, His forced journeyings to and fro, His blows and wounds, His scourging, the crown of thorns, the nails, the Cross. They are all summed up in the Crucifix itself, as it meets our eyes; they are represented all at once on His sacred flesh, as it hangs up before us — and meditation is made easy by the spectacle. It is otherwise with the sufferings of His soul; they cannot be painted for us, nor can they even be duly investigated: they are beyond both sense and thought; and yet they anticipated His bodily sufferings. The agony, a pain of the soul, not of the body, was the first act of His tremendous sacrifice; "My soul is sorrowful even unto death,"[27] He said; nay; if He suffered in the body, it really was in the soul, for the body did but convey the infliction on to that which was the true recipient and seat of the suffering.

This it is very much to the purpose to insist upon; I say, it was not the body that suffered, but the soul in the body; it was the soul and not the body which was the seat of the suffering of the Eternal Word. Consider, then, there is no real pain, though there may be apparent suffering, when there is no kind of inward sensibility or spirit to be the seat of it. A tree, for instance, has life, organs, growth, and decay; it may be wounded and injured; it droops, and is killed; but it does not suffer, because it has no mind or sensible principle within it. But wherever this gift of an immaterial principle is found, there pain is possible, and greater pain according to the quality of the gift. Had we no spirit of any kind, we should feel as little as a tree feels; had we no soul, we should not feel pain more acutely than a brute feels it; but, being

---

27. Matthew 26:38.

men, we feel pain in a way in which none but those who have souls can feel it.

Living beings, I say, feel more or less according to the spirit which is in them; brutes feel far less than man, because they cannot reflect on what they feel; they have no advertence or direct consciousness of their sufferings. This it is that makes pain so trying, viz., that we cannot help thinking of it, while we suffer it. It is before us, it possesses the mind, it keeps our thoughts fixed upon it. Whatever draws the mind off the thought of it lessens it; hence friends try to amuse us when we are in pain, for amusement is a diversion. If the pain is slight, they sometimes succeed with us; and then we are, so to say, without pain, even while we suffer. And hence it continually happens that in violent exercise or labor, men meet with blows or cuts, so considerable and so durable in their effect, as to bear witness to the suffering which must have attended their infliction, of which nevertheless they recollect nothing. And in quarrels and in battles wounds are received which, from the excitement of the moment, are brought home to the consciousness of the combatant, not by the pain at the time of receiving them, but by the loss of blood that follows.

I will show you presently, my brethren, how I mean to apply what I have said to the consideration of our Lord's sufferings; first I will make another remark. Consider, then, that hardly any one stroke of pain is intolerable; it is intolerable when it continues. You cry out perhaps that you cannot bear more; patients feel as if they could stop the surgeon's hand, simply because he continues to pain them. Their feeling is that they have borne *as much* as they can bear; as if the continuance and not the intenseness was what made it too much for them. What does this mean, but that the memory of the foregoing moments of pain acts upon and (as it were) edges the pain that succeeds? If the third or fourth or twentieth moment of pain could be taken by itself, if the succession of the moments that preceded it could be forgotten, it would be no more than the first moment, as bearable as the first (taking away the shock which accompanies the first); but what makes it unbearable is that it *is* the twentieth; that the first, the second, the third, on to the nineteenth moment of pain, are all concentrated in the twentieth; so that every additional moment of pain has all the force, the ever-increasing force, of all that has preceded it. Hence, I repeat, it is that brute animals would seem to feel so little pain, because, that is, they have not the power of reflection or of consciousness. They do not know they exist; they do not contemplate themselves; they do not look backward or forward; every moment as it succeeds is their all; they wander over the face of the earth, and see this thing and that, and feel pleasure and pain, but still they take everything as it comes, and then let it go again, as men do in dreams. They have memory, but not the memory of an intellectual being; they put together nothing, they make nothing properly one and individual to themselves out of the particular sensations which they receive; nothing is to them a reality, or has a substance, beyond those sensations; they are but sensible of a number of successive impressions. And hence, as their other feelings, so their feeling of pain is but faint and dull, in spite of their outward manifestations of it. It is the intellectual comprehension of pain, as a whole diffused through successive moments, which gives it its special power and keenness, and it is the soul only, which a brute has not, which is capable of that comprehension.

Now apply this to the sufferings of our Lord; do you recollect their offering Him wine mingled with myrrh, when He was on the point of being crucified? He would not drink of it; why? Because such a portion would have stupefied His mind, and He was bent on bearing the pain in all its bitterness. You see from this, my brethren, the character of His sufferings; He would have fain escaped them, had that been His Father's will; "If it be possible," He said, "let this chalice pass from Me"; but since it was not possible, He says calmly and decidedly to the Apostle, who would have rescued Him from suffering, "The chalice which My Father hath given Me, shall I not drink it?"[28] If He was to suffer, He gave Himself to suffering; He did not come to suffer as little as He could; He did not turn away His face from the suffering; He confronted it, or, as I may say, He breasted it, that every particular portion of it might make its due impression on Him. And as men are superior to brute animals, and are affected by pain more than they, by reason of the mind within them, which gives a substance to pain, such as it cannot have in the instance of brutes; so, in like manner, our Lord felt pain of the body, with an advertence and a consciousness, and therefore with a keenness and intensity, and with a unity of perception, which none of us can possibly fathom or compass, because His soul was so absolutely in His power, so simply free from the influence of distractions, so fully directed upon the pain, so utterly surrendered, so simply subjected to the suffering. And thus He may truly be said to have suffered the whole of His passion in every moment of it.

Recollect that our Blessed Lord was in this respect different from us, that, though He was perfect man, yet there was a power in Him greater than His soul, which ruled His soul, for He was God. The soul of other men is subjected to its own wishes, feelings, impulses, passions, perturbations; His soul was subjected simply to His Eternal and Divine Personality. Nothing happened to His soul by chance, or on a sudden; He never was taken by surprise; nothing affected Him without His willing beforehand that it should affect Him. Never did He sorrow, or fear, or desire, or rejoice in spirit, but He first willed to be sorrowful, or afraid, or desirous, or joyful. When we suffer, it is because outward agents and the uncontrollable emotions of our minds bring suffering upon us. We are brought under the discipline of pain

---

28. John 18:11.

involuntarily, we suffer from it more or less acutely according to accidental circumstances, we find our patience more or less tried by it according to our state of mind, and we do our best to provide alleviations or remedies of it. We cannot anticipate beforehand how much of it will come upon us, or how far we shall be able to sustain it; nor can we say afterward why we have felt just what we have felt, or why we did not bear the suffering better. It was otherwise with our Lord. His Divine Person was not subject, could not be exposed, to the influence of His own human affections and feelings, except so far as He chose. I repeat, when He chose to fear, He feared; when He chose to be angry, He was angry; when He chose to grieve, He was grieved. He was not open to emotion, but He opened upon Himself voluntarily the impulse by which He was moved. Consequently, when He determined to suffer the pain of His vicarious passion, whatever He did, He did, as the Wise Man says, *instanter*, "earnestly," with His might; He did not do it by halves; He did not turn away His mind from the suffering as we do (how should He, who came to suffer, who could not have suffered but of His own act?), no, He did not say and unsay, do and undo; He said and He did; He said, "Lo, I come to do Thy will, O God; sacrifice and offering Thou wouldest not, but a body hast Thou fitted to Me."[29] He took a body in order that He might suffer; He became man, that He might suffer as man; and when His hour was come, that hour of Satan and of darkness, the hour when sin was to pour its full malignity upon Him, it followed that He offered Himself wholly, a holocaust, a whole burnt-offering; as the whole of His body, stretched out upon the Cross, so the whole of His soul, His whole advertence, His whole consciousness, a mind awake, a sense acute, a living cooperation, a present, absolute intention, not a virtual permission, not a heartless submission, this did He

---

29. Hebrews 10:5.

present to His tormentors. His passion was an action; He lived most energetically, while He lay languishing, fainting, and dying. Nor did He die, except by an act of the will; for He bowed His head, in command as well as in resignation, and said, "Father, into Thy hands I commend My Spirit"[30]; He gave the word, He surrendered His soul, He did not lose it.

Thus you see, my brethren, had our Lord only suffered in the body, and in it not so much as other men, still as regards the pain, He would have really suffered indefinitely more, because pain is to be measured by the power of realizing it. God was the sufferer; God suffered in His human nature; the sufferings belonged to God, and were drunk up, were drained out to the bottom of the chalice, because God drank them; not tasted or sipped, not flavored, disguised by human medicaments, as man disposes of the cup of anguish. And what I have been saying will further serve to answer an objection, which I shall proceed to notice, and which perhaps exists latently in the minds of many, and leads them to overlook the part which our Lord's soul had in His gracious satisfaction for sin.

Our Lord said, when His agony was commencing, "My soul is sorrowful unto death"[31]; now you may ask, my brethren, whether He had not certain consolations peculiar to Himself, impossible in any other, which diminished or impeded the distress of His soul, and caused Him to feel, not more, but less than an ordinary man. For instance, He had a sense of innocence which no other sufferer could have; even His persecutors, even the false apostle who betrayed Him, the judge who sentenced Him, and the soldiers who conducted the execution, testified His innocence. "I have condemned the innocent blood," said Judas; "I am clear from the blood of this just Person," said Pilate; "Truly this was a

---

30. Luke 23:46.
31. Matthew 26:38.

just Man," cried the centurion.[32] And if even they, sinners, bore witness to His sinlessness, how much more did His own soul! And we know well that even in our own case, sinners as we are, on the consciousness of innocence or of guilt mainly turns our power of enduring opposition and calumny; how much more, you will say, in the case of our Lord, did the sense of inward sanctity compensate for the suffering and annihilate the shame! Again, you may say that He knew that His sufferings would be short, and that their issue would be joyful, whereas uncertainty of the future is the keenest element of human distress; but He could not have anxiety, for He was not in suspense; nor despondency or despair, for He never was deserted. And in confirmation you may refer to St. Paul, who expressly tells us that, "for the joy set before Him," our Lord "despised the shame." And certainly there is a marvelous calm and self-possession in all He does: consider His warning to the Apostles, "Watch and pray, lest ye enter into temptation; the spirit indeed is willing, but the flesh is weak"; or His words to Judas, "Friend, wherefore art thou come?" and, "Judas, betrayest thou the Son of Man with a kiss?" Or to Peter, "All that take the sword shall perish with the sword"[33]; or to the man who struck Him, "If I have spoken evil, bear witness of the evil; but if well, why smitest thou Me?"[34] Or to His Mother, "Woman, behold thy Son."[35]

All this is true and much to be insisted on; but it quite agrees with, or rather illustrates, what I have been observing. My brethren, you have only said (to use a human phrase) that He was always Himself. His mind was its own center, and was never in the slightest degree thrown off its heavenly and most perfect balance. What He suffered, He suffered because He put Himself

---

32. Matthew 27:4; 27:24; Luke 23:47.
33. Matthew 26.
34. John 18:23.
35. John 19:26.

under suffering, and that deliberately and calmly. As He said to the leper, "I will, be thou clean"; and to the paralytic, "Thy sins be forgiven thee"; and to the centurion, "I will come and heal him"; and of Lazarus, "I go to wake him out of sleep"; so He said, "Now I will begin to suffer," and He did begin. His composure is but the proof how entirely He governed His own mind. He drew back, at the proper moment, the bolts and fastenings, and opened the gates, and the floods fell right upon His soul in all their fullness. That is what St. Mark tells us of Him; and he is said to have written his Gospels from the very mouth of St. Peter, who was one of three witnesses present at the time. "They came," he says, "to the place which is called Gethsemani; and He saith to His disciples, Sit you here while I pray. And He taketh with Him Peter and James and John, and He *began to be* frightened and to be very heavy." You see how deliberately He acts; He comes to a certain spot; and then, giving the word of command, and withdrawing the support of the Godhead from His soul, distress, terror, and dejection at once rush in upon it. Thus He walks forth into a mental agony with as definite an action as if it were some bodily torture, the fire or the wheel.

This being the case, you will see at once, my brethren, that it is nothing to the purpose to say that He would be supported under His trial by the consciousness of innocence and the anticipation of triumph; for His trial consisted in the withdrawal, as of other causes of consolation, so of that very consciousness and anticipation. The same act of the will which admitted the influence upon His soul of any distress at all, admitted all distresses at once. It was not the contest between antagonist impulses and views, coming from without, but the operation of an inward resolution. As men of self-command can turn from one thought to another at their will, so much more did He deliberately deny Himself the comfort and satiate Himself with the woe. In that moment His soul thought not of the future, He thought only of the present burden which was upon Him, and which He had come upon earth to sustain.

And now, my brethren, what was it He had to bear, when He thus opened upon His soul the torrent of this predestinated pain? Alas! He had to bear what is well known to us, what is familiar to us, but what to Him was woe unutterable. He had to bear that which is so easy a thing to us, so natural, so welcome, that we cannot conceive of it as of a great endurance, but which to Him had the scent and the poison of death — He had, my dear brethren, to bear the weight of sin; He had to bear your sins; He had to bear the sins of the whole world. Sin is an easy thing to us; we think little of it; we do not understand how the Creator can think much of it; we cannot bring our imagination to believe that it deserves retribution, and, when even in this world punishments follow upon it, we explain them away or turn our minds from them. But consider what sin is in itself; it is rebellion against God; it is a traitor's act who aims at the overthrow and death of His sovereign; it is that, if I may use a strong expression, which, could the Divine Governor of the world cease to be, would be sufficient to bring it about. Sin is the mortal enemy of the All-holy, so that He and it cannot be together; and as the All-holy drives it from His presence into the outer darkness, so, if God could be less than God, it is sin that would have power to make Him less. And here observe, my brethren, that when once Almighty Love, by taking flesh, entered this created system, and submitted Himself to its laws, then forthwith this antagonist of good and truth, taking advantage of the opportunity, flew at that flesh which He had taken, and fixed on it, and was its death. The envy of the Pharisees, the treachery of Judas, and the madness of the people, were but the instrument or the expression of the enmity which sin felt toward Eternal Purity as soon as, in infinite mercy toward men, He put Himself within its reach. Sin could not touch His Divine Majesty; but it could assail Him in that way in which He allowed Himself to be assailed, that is, through the medium of His humanity. And in the issue, in the death of God incarnate, you are but taught, my brethren, what sin is in itself, and what it was which then was falling, in its hour and in its strength, upon His human nature, when He allowed that nature to be so filled with horror and dismay at the very anticipation.

There, then, in that most awful hour, knelt the Savior of the world, putting off the defenses of His divinity, dismissing His reluctant Angels, who in myriads were ready at His call, and opening His arms, baring His breast, sinless as He was, to the assault of His foe — of a foe whose breath was a pestilence, and whose embrace was an agony. There He knelt, motionless and still, while the vile and horrible fiend clad His spirit in a robe steeped in all that is hateful and heinous in human crime, which clung close round His heart, and filled His conscience, and found its way into every sense and pore of His mind, and spread over Him a moral leprosy, till He almost felt Himself to be that which He never could be, and which His foe would fain have made Him. Oh, the horror, when He looked, and did not know Himself, and felt as a foul and loathsome sinner, from His vivid perception of that mass of corruption which poured over His head and ran down even to the skirts of His garments! Oh, the distraction, when He found His eyes, and hands, and feet, and lips, and heart, as if the members of the Evil One, and not of God! Are these the hands of the Immaculate Lamb of God, once innocent, but now red with ten thousand barbarous deeds of blood? Are these His lips, not uttering prayer, and praise, and holy blessings, but as if defiled with oaths, and blasphemies, and doctrines of devils? Or His eyes, profaned as they are by all the evil visions and idolatrous fascinations for which men have abandoned their adorable Creator? And His ears, they ring with sounds of revelry and of strife; and His heart is frozen with avarice, and cruelty, and unbelief; and His very memory is laden with every sin which has been committed since the fall, in all regions of the earth, with the pride of the old giants, and the lusts of the five cities, and the obduracy of Egypt, and the ambition of Babel, and the unthankfulness and scorn of Israel. Oh, who does not know the misery of a haunting thought which comes again and again, in spite of rejection, to annoy, if it cannot seduce? Or of some odious and sickening imagination, in no sense one's own, but forced upon the mind from without? Or of evil knowledge, gained with or without a man's fault, but which he would give a great price to be rid of at once and for ever? And adversaries such as these gather around Thee, Blessed Lord, in millions now; they come in troops more numerous than the locust or the palmer-worm, or the plagues of hail, and flies, and frogs, which were sent against Pharaoh. Of the living and of the dead and of the as yet unborn, of the lost and of the saved, of Thy people and of strangers, of sinners and of saints, all sins are there. Thy dearest are there, Thy saints and Thy chosen are upon Thee; Thy three Apostles, Peter, James, and John; but not as comforters, but as accusers, like the friends of Job, "sprinkling dust towards heaven,"[36] and heaping curses on Thy head. All are there but one; one only is not there, one only; for she who had no part in sin, she only could console Thee, and therefore she is not nigh. She will be near Thee on the Cross, she is separated from Thee in the garden. She has been Thy companion and Thy confidant through Thy life, she interchanged with Thee the pure thoughts and holy meditations of thirty years; but her virgin ear may not take in, nor may her immaculate heart conceive, what now is in vision before Thee. None was equal to the weight but God; sometimes before Thy saints Thou hast brought the image of a single sin, as it appears in the light of Thy countenance, or of venial sins, not mortal; and they have told us that the sight did all but kill them, nay,

---

36. Job 2:12.

would have killed them, had it not been instantly withdrawn. The Mother of God, for all her sanctity, nay by reason of it, could not have borne even one brood of that innumerable progeny of Satan which now compasses Thee about. It is the long history of a world, and God alone can bear the load of it. Hopes blighted, vows broken, lights quenched, warnings scorned, opportunities lost; the innocent betrayed, the young hardened, the penitent relapsing, the just overcome, the aged failing; the sophistry of misbelief, the willfulness of passion, the obduracy of pride, the tyranny of habit, the canker of remorse, the wasting fever of care, the anguish of shame, the pining of disappointment, the sickness of despair; such cruel, such pitiable spectacles, such heartrending, revolting, detestable, maddening scenes; nay, the haggard faces, the convulsed lips, the flushed cheek, the dark brow of the willing slaves of evil, they are all before Him now; they are upon Him and in Him. They are with Him instead of that ineffable peace which has inhabited His soul since the moment of His conception. They are upon Him, they are all but His own; He cries to His Father as if He were the criminal, not the victim; His agony takes the form of guilt and compunction. He is doing penance, He is making confession, He is exercising contrition, with a reality and a virtue infinitely greater than that of all saints and penitents together; for He is the One Victim for us all, the sole Satisfaction, the real Penitent, all but the real sinner.

He rises languidly from the earth and turns around to meet the traitor and his band, now quickly nearing the deep shade. He turns, and lo there is blood upon His garment and in His footprints. Whence come these first-fruits of the passion of the Lamb? No soldier's scourge has touched His shoulders, nor the hangman's nails His hands and feet. My brethren, He has bled before His time; He has shed blood; yes, and it is His agonizing soul which has broken up His framework of flesh and poured it forth. His passion has begun from within. That tormented Heart, the seat of tenderness and love, began at length to labor and to beat with vehemence beyond its nature; "the foundations of the great deep were broken up"; the red streams rushed forth so copious and fierce as to overflow the veins, and bursting through the pores, they stood in a thick dew over His whole skin; then forming into drops, they rolled down full and heavy, and drenched the ground.

"My soul is sorrowful even unto death," He said. It has been said of that dreadful pestilence which now is upon us, that it begins with death; by which is meant that it has no stage or crisis, that hope is over when it comes, and that what looks like its course is but the death agony and the process of dissolution; and thus our Atoning Sacrifice, in a much higher sense, began with this passion of woe, and only did not die, because at His Omnipotent will His Heart did not break, nor Soul separate from Body, till He had suffered on the Cross.

No; He has not yet exhausted that full chalice, from which at first His natural infirmity shrank. The seizure and the arraignment, and the buffeting, and the prison, and the trial, and the mocking, and the passing to and fro, and the scourging, and the crown of thorns, and the slow march to Calvary, and the crucifixion, these are all to come. A night and a day, hour after hour, is slowly to run out before the end comes, and the satisfaction is completed.

And then, when the appointed moment arrived, and He gave the word, as His passion had begun with His soul, with the soul did it end. He did not die of bodily exhaustion, or of bodily pain; at His will His tormented Heart broke, and He commended His Spirit to the Father.

*   *   *   *   *   *

"O Heart of Jesus, all Love, I offer Thee these humble prayers for myself, and for all those who unite themselves with me in Spirit to adore Thee. O holiest Heart of Jesus most lovely, I intend to renew and to offer to Thee these acts of adoration and these prayers, for myself a wretched sinner, and for all those who are associated with me in Thy adoration, through all moments while I breathe, even to the end of my life. I recommend to Thee, O my Jesus, Holy Church, Thy dear spouse and our true Mother, all just souls and all poor sinners, the afflicted, the dying, and all mankind. Let not Thy Blood be shed for them in vain. Finally, deign to apply it in relief of the souls in Purgatory, of those in particular who have practiced in the course of their life this holy devotion of adoring Thee."

Intellect, the Instrument of Religious Training

In *Sermons Preached on Various Occasions.*
Preached on the Feast of St. Monica, Sunday after
Ascension, 1856, in the University Church, Dublin

"And when He came nigh to the gate of the city, behold, a dead man was carried out, the only son of his mother: and she was a widow." Luke 7:12

This day we celebrate one of the most remarkable feasts in the calendar. We commemorate a Saint who gained the heavenly crown by prayers indeed and tears, by sleepless nights and weary wanderings, but not in the administration of any high office in the Church, not in the fulfilment of some great resolution or special counsel; not as a preacher, teacher, evangelist, reformer, or champion of the faith; not as Bishop of the flock, or temporal governor; not by eloquence, by wisdom, or by controversial success; not in the way of any other saint whom we invoke in the circle of the year; but as a mother, seeking and gaining by her penances the conversion of her son. It was for no ordinary son that she prayed, and it was no ordinary supplication by which she gained him. When a holy man saw its vehemence, ere it was successful, he said to her, "Go in peace; the son of such prayers cannot perish." The prediction was fulfilled beyond its letter; not only was that young man converted, but after his conversion he became a saint; not only a saint, but a doctor also, and "instructed many unto justice." St. Augustine was the son for whom she prayed; and if he has been a luminary for all ages of the Church since, many thanks do we owe to his mother, St. Monica, who having borne him in the flesh, travailed for him in the spirit.

The Church, in her choice of a gospel for this feast, has likened St. Monica to the desolate widow whom our Lord met at the gate of the city, as she was going forth to bury the corpse of her only son. He saw her, and said, "Weep not"; and he touched the bier, and the dead arose. St. Monica asked and obtained a more noble miracle. Many a mother who is anxious for her son's bodily welfare, neglects his soul. So did not the Saint of today; her son might be accomplished, eloquent, able, and distinguished; all this was nothing to her while he was dead in God's sight, while he was the slave of sin, while he was the prey of heresy. She desired his true life. She wearied heaven with prayer, and wore out herself with praying; she did not at once prevail. He left his home; he was carried forward by his four bearers, ignorance, pride, appetite, and ambition; he was carried out into a foreign land, he crossed over from Africa to Italy. She followed him, she followed the corpse, the chief, the only mourner; she went where he went, from city to city. It was nothing to her to leave her dear home and her native soil; she had no country below; her sole rest, her sole repose, her *Nunc dimittis*,[37] was his new birth. So while she still walked forth in her deep anguish and isolation, and her silent prayer, she was at length rewarded by the long-coveted miracle. Grace melted the proud heart, and purified the corrupt breast of Augustine, and restored and comforted his mother; and hence, in today's Collect, the Almighty Giver is especially addressed as "*Mœrentium consolator et in Te sperantium salus*"; the consoler of those that mourn, and the health of those who hope.

And thus Monica, as the widow in the gospel, becomes an image of Holy Church, who is ever lamenting over her lost children, and by her importunate prayers, ever recovering them from the grave of sin; and to Monica, as the Church's representative, may be addressed those words of the Prophet: "Put off, O Jerusalem, the garments of thy mourning and affliction; arise, and look about towards the East, and behold thy children; for they went out from thee on foot, led by the enemies; but the Lord will bring them to thee exalted with honor, as children of the kingdom."[38]

This, I say, is not a history of past time merely, but of every age. Generation passes after generation, and there is on the one side the same doleful, dreary wandering, the same feverish unrest, the same fleeting enjoyments, the same abiding and hopeless misery; and on the other, the same anxiously beating heart of impotent affection. Age goes after age, and still Augustine rushes forth again and again, with his young ambition, and his intellectual energy, and his turbulent appetites; educated, yet untaught; with powers strengthened, sharpened, refined by exercise, but unenlightened and untrained — goes forth into the world, ardent, self-willed, reckless, headstrong, inexperienced, to fall into the hands of those who seek his life, and to become the victim of heresy and sin. And

---

37. This is the Latin title for the Canticle of Simeon, Luke 2:29–32.
38. Baruch 5:1–6.

still, again and again does hapless Monica weep; weeping for that dear child who grew up with her from the womb, and of whom she is now robbed; of whom she has lost sight; wandering with him in his wanderings, following his steps in her imagination, cherishing his image in her heart, keeping his name upon her lips, and feeling withal, that, as a woman, she is unable to cope with the violence and the artifices of the world. And still again and again does Holy Church take her part and her place, with a heart as tender and more strong, with an arm, and an eye, and an intellect more powerful than hers, with an influence more than human, more sagacious than the world, and more religious than home, to restrain and reclaim those whom passion, or example, or sophistry is hurrying forward to destruction.

My Brethren, there is something happy in the circumstance, that the first Sunday of our academical worship should fall on the feast of St. Monica. For is not this one chief aspect of a University, and an aspect which it especially bears in this sacred place, to supply that which that memorable Saint so much desiderated, and for which she attempted to compensate by her prayers? Is it not one part of our especial office to receive those from the hands of father and mother, whom father and mother can keep no longer? Thus, while professing all sciences, and speaking by the mouths of philosophers and sages, a University delights in the well-known appellation of "Alma Mater." She is a mother who, after the pattern of that greatest and most heavenly of mothers, is, on the one hand, "*Mater Amabilis*," and "*Causa nostræ lætitiæ*," and on the other, "*Sedes Sapientiæ*"[39] also. She is a mother, living, not in the seclusion of the family, and in the garden's shade, but in the wide world, in the populous and busy town, claiming, like our great Mother, the meek and tender Mary, "to praise her own self, and to glory, and to open her mouth," because she alone has

---

39. Mother Most Loveable, Cause of Our Joy, and Seat of Wisdom are all titles of the Blessed Virgin Mary found in the Litany of Loreto.

"compassed the circuit of Heaven, and penetrated into the bottom of the deep, and walked upon the waves of the sea," and in every department of human learning, is able to confute and put right those who would set knowledge against itself, and would make truth contradict truth, and would persuade the world that, to be religious, you must be ignorant, and to be intellectual, you must be unbelieving.

My meaning will be clearer, if I revert to the nature and condition of the human mind. The human mind, as you know, my Brethren, may be regarded from two principal points of view, as intellectual and as moral. As intellectual, it apprehends truth; as moral, it apprehends duty. The perfection of the intellect is called ability and talent; the perfection of our moral nature is virtue. And it is our great misfortune here, and our trial, that, as things are found in the world, the two are separated, and independent of each other; that, where power of intellect is, there need not be virtue; and that where right, and goodness, and moral greatness are, there need not be talent. It was not so in the beginning; not that our nature is essentially different from what it was when first created; but that the Creator, upon its creation, raised it above itself by a supernatural grace, which blended together all its faculties, and made them conspire into one whole, and act in common toward one end; so that, had the race continued in that blessed state of privilege, there never would have been distance, rivalry, hostility between one faculty and another. It is otherwise now; so much the worse for us — the grace is gone; the soul cannot hold together; it falls to pieces; its elements strive with each other. And as, when a kingdom has long been in a state of tumult, sedition, or rebellion, certain portions break off from the whole and from the central government and set up for themselves; so is it with the soul of man. So is it, I say, with the soul, long ago — that a number of small kingdoms, independent of each other and at war with each other, have arisen in it, such and so many as to reduce the original sovereignty to a circuit of territory and to an influence not more considerable than they have themselves. And all these small dominions, as I may call them, in the soul, are, of course, one by one, incomplete and defective, strong in some points, weak in others, because not any one of them is the whole, sufficient for itself, but only one part of the whole, which, on the contrary, is made up of all the faculties of the soul together. Hence you find in one man, or one set of men, the reign, I may call it, the acknowledged reign of passion or appetite; among others, the avowed reign of brute strength and material resources; among others, the reign of intellect; and among others (and would they were many!) the more excellent reign of virtue. Such is the state of things, as it shows to us, when we cast our eyes abroad into the world; and everyone, when he comes to years of discretion, and begins to think, has all these separate powers warring in his own breast — appetite, passion, secular ambition, intellect, and conscience, and trying severally to get possession of him. And when he looks out of himself, he sees them all severally embodied on a grand scale, in large establishments and centers, outside of him, one here and another there, in aid of that importunate canvass, so to express myself, which each of them is carrying on within him. And thus, at least for a time, he is in a state of internal strife, confusion, and uncertainty, first attracted this way, then that, not knowing how to choose, though sooner or later choose he must; or rather, he must choose soon, and cannot choose late, for he cannot help thinking, speaking, and acting; and to think, speak, and act, is to choose.

This is a very serious state of things; and what makes it worse is, that these various faculties and powers of the human mind have so long been separated from each other, so long cultivated and developed each by itself, that it comes to be taken for granted that they cannot be united; and it is commonly thought, because some men follow duty, others pleasure, others glory, and others intellect, therefore that one of these things excludes the other; that duty cannot be pleasant, that virtue cannot be intellectual, that goodness cannot be great, that conscientiousness cannot be heroic; and the fact is often so, I grant, that there *is* a separation, though I deny its necessity. I grant, that, from the disorder and confusion into which the human mind has fallen, too often good men are not attractive, and bad men are; too often cleverness, or wit, or taste, or richness of fancy, or keenness of intellect, or depth, or knowledge, or pleasantness and agreeableness, is on the side of error and not on the side of virtue. Excellence, as things are, does lie, I grant, in more directions than one, and it is ever easier to excel in one thing than in two. If then a man has more talent, there is the chance that he will have less goodness; if he is careful about his religious duties, there is the chance he is behind-hand in general knowledge; and in matter of fact, in particular cases, persons may be found, correct and virtuous, who are heavy, narrow-minded, and unintellectual, and again, unprincipled men, who are brilliant and amusing. And thus you see, my Brethren, how that particular temptation comes about, of which I speak, when boyhood is past, and youth is opening; not only is the soul plagued and tormented by the thousand temptations which rise up within it, but it is exposed moreover to the sophistry of the Evil One, whispering that duty and religion are very right indeed, admirable, supernatural — who doubts it? — but that, somehow or other, religious people are commonly either very dull or very tiresome: nay, that religion itself after all is more suitable to women and children, who live at home, than to men.

O my Brethren, do you not confess to the truth of much of what I have been saying? Is it not so, that, when your mind began to open, in proportion as it opened, it was by that very opening made rebellious against what you knew to be duty? In matter of fact, was not your intellect in league with disobedience? Instead of uniting knowledge and religion, as you might have done, did you not set one against the other? For instance, was it not one of the first voluntary exercises of your mind, to indulge a wrong curiosity? A curiosity which you confessed to yourselves to be wrong, which went against your conscience, while you indulged it. You desired to know a number of things, which it could do you no good to know. This is how boys begin; as soon as their mind begins to stir, it looks the wrong way, and runs upon what is evil. This is their first wrong step; and their next use of their intellect is to put what is evil into words: This is their second wrong step. They form images, and entertain thoughts, which should be away, and they stamp them upon themselves and others by expressing them. And next, the bad turn which they do to others, others retaliate on them. One wrong speech provokes another; and thus there grows up among them from boyhood that miserable tone of conversation — hinting and suggesting evil, jesting, bantering on the subject of sin, supplying fuel for the inflammable imagination — which lasts through life, which is wherever the world is, which is the very breath of the world, which the world cannot do without, which the world "speaks out of the abundance of its heart," and which you may prophesy will prevail in every ordinary assemblage of men, as soon as they are at their ease and begin to talk freely — a sort of vocal worship of the Evil One, to which the Evil One listens with special satisfaction, because he looks on it as the preparation for worse sin; for from bad thoughts and bad words proceed bad deeds.

Bad company creates a distaste for good; and hence it happens that, when a youth has gone the length I have been supposing, he is repelled, from that very distaste, from those places and scenes which would do him good. He begins to lose the delight he once had in going home. By little and little he loses his enjoyment in the pleasant countenances, and untroubled smiles, and gentle ways, of that family circle which is so dear to him still. At first he says to himself that he is not worthy of them, and therefore keeps away; but at length the routine of home is tiresome to him. He has aspirations and ambitions which home does not satisfy. He wants more than home can give. His curiosity now takes a new turn; he listens to views and discussions which are inconsistent with the sanctity of religious faith. At first he has no temptation to adopt them; only he wishes to know what is "said." As time goes on, however, living with companions who have no fixed principle, and who, if they do not oppose, at least do not take for granted, any the most elementary truths; or worse, hearing or reading what is directly against religion, at length, without being conscious of it, he admits a skeptical influence upon his mind. He does not know it, he does not recognize it, but there it is; and, *before* he recognizes it, it leads him to a fretful, impatient way of speaking of the persons, conduct, words, and measures of religious men or of men in authority. This is the way in which he relieves his mind of the burden which is growing heavier and heavier every day. And so he goes on, approximating more and more closely to sceptics and infidels, and feeling more and more congeniality with their modes of thinking, till someday suddenly, from some accident, the fact breaks upon him, and he sees clearly that he is an unbeliever himself.

He can no longer conceal from himself that he does not believe, and a sharp anguish darts through him, and for a time he is made miserable; next, he *laments* indeed that former undoubting faith, which he has lost, but as some pleasant dream; a dream, though a pleasant one, from which he has been awakened, but which, however pleasant, *he* forsooth, cannot help *being* a dream. And his next stage is to experience a great expansion and elevation of mind; for his field of view is swept clear of all that filled it from childhood, and now he may build up for himself anything he pleases instead. So he begins to form his own ideas of things, and these please and satisfy him for a time; then he gets used to them, and tires of them, and he takes up others; and now he has begun that everlasting round of seeking and never finding: At length, after various trials, he gives up the search altogether, and decides that nothing can be known, and there is no such thing as truth, and that if anything is to be professed, the creed he started from is as good as any other, and has more claims — however, that really nothing is true, nothing is certain. Or, if he be of a more ardent temperature, or, like Augustine, the object of God's special mercy, then he cannot give up the inquiry, though he has no chance of solving it, and he roams about, "walking through dry places, seeking rest, and finding none."[40] Meanwhile poor Monica sees the change in its effects, though she does not estimate it in itself, or know exactly what it is, or how it came about: nor, even though it be told her, can she enter into it, or understand how one, so dear to her, can be subjected to it. But a dreadful change there is, and she perceives it too clearly; a dreadful change for him and for her; a wall of separation has grown up between them: She cannot throw it down again; but she can turn to her God, and weep and pray.

Now, my Brethren, observe, the strength of this delusion lies in there being a sort of truth in it. Young men feel a consciousness of certain faculties within them which demand exercise, aspirations which must have an object, for which they do not commonly find exercise or object in religious circles. This want is no excuse for them, if they think, say, or do anything against faith or morals: But still it is the occasion of their sinning. It is the fact, they are not only moral, they are intellectual beings; but, ever since the fall of man, religion is here, and philosophy is there; each has its own centers of influence, separate from the other; intellectual men desiderate something in the homes of religion, and religious men desiderate something in the schools of science.

---

40. Matthew 12:43.

Here, then, I conceive, is the object of the Holy See and the Catholic Church in setting up Universities; it is to reunite things which were in the beginning joined together by God, and have been put asunder by man. Some persons will say that I am thinking of confining, distorting, and stunting the growth of the intellect by ecclesiastical supervision. I have no such thought. Nor have I any thought of a compromise, as if religion must give up something, and science something. I wish the intellect to range with the utmost freedom, and religion to enjoy an equal freedom; but what I am stipulating for is, that they should be found in one and the same place and exemplified in the same persons. I want to destroy that diversity of centers, which puts everything into confusion by creating a contrariety of influences. I wish the same spots and the same individuals to be at once oracles of philosophy and shrines of devotion. It will not satisfy me, what satisfies so many, to have two independent systems, intellectual and religious, going at once side by side, by a sort of division of labor, and only accidentally brought together. It will not satisfy me, if religion is here, and science there, and young men converse with science all day, and lodge with religion in the evening. It is not touching the evil, to which these remarks have been directed, if young men eat and drink and sleep in one place and think in another: I want the same roof to contain both the intellectual and moral discipline. Devotion is not a sort of finish given to the sciences; nor is science a sort of feather in the cap, if I may so express myself, an ornament and set-off to devotion. I want the intellectual layman to be religious, and the devout ecclesiastic to be intellectual.

This is no matter of terms, nor of subtle distinctions. Sanctity has its influence; intellect has its influence; the influence of sanctity is the greater on the long run; the influence of intellect is greater at the moment. Therefore, in the case of the young, whose education lasts a few years, where the intellect is, *there* is the influence. Their literary, their scientific teachers, really have the forming of them. Let both influences act freely, and then, as a general rule, no system of mere religious guardianship which neglects the Reason, will in matter of fact succeed against the School. Youths need a masculine religion, if it is to carry captive their restless imaginations, and their wild intellects, as well as to touch their susceptible hearts.

Look down then upon us from Heaven, O blessed Monica, for we are engaged in supplying that very want which called for thy prayers and gained for thee thy crown. Thou who didst obtain thy son's conversion by the merit of thy intercession, continue that intercession for us, that we may be blest, as human instruments, in the use of those human means by which ordinarily the Holy Cross is raised aloft, and religion commands the world. Gain for us, first, that we may intensely feel that God's grace is all in all, and that we are nothing; next, that, for His greater glory, and for the honor of Holy Church, and for the good of man, we may be "zealous for all the better gifts,"[41] and may excel in intellect as we excel in virtue.

---

41. 1 Corinthians 12:31.

The Theory of Developments in Religious Doctrine (excerpt)

In *Sermons Chiefly on the Theory of Religious Belief,*
Preached Before the University of Oxford (1843)

"But Mary kept all these things, and pondered them in her heart."
Luke 2:19

Little is told us in Scripture concerning the Blessed Virgin, but there is one grace of which the Evangelists make her the pattern, in a few simple sentences — of Faith. Zacharias questioned the Angel's message, but "Mary said, Behold the handmaid of the

Lord; be it unto me according to thy word."[42] Accordingly Elisabeth, speaking with an apparent allusion to the contrast thus exhibited between her own highly-favored husband, righteous Zacharias, and the still more highly-favored Mary, said, on receiving her salutation, "Blessed art thou among women, and blessed is the fruit of thy womb; Blessed is she that believed, for there shall be a performance of those things which were told her from the Lord."[43]

2. But Mary's faith did not end in a mere acquiescence in Divine providences and revelations: As the text informs us, she "pondered" them. When the shepherds came, and told of the vision of Angels which they had seen at the time of the Nativity, and how one of them announced that the Infant in her arms was "the Savior, which is Christ the Lord," while others did but wonder, "Mary kept all these things, and pondered them in her heart."[44] Again, when her Son and Savior had come to the age of twelve years, and had left her for awhile for His Father's service, and had been found, to her surprise, in the Temple, amid the doctors, both hearing them and asking them questions, and had, on her addressing Him, vouchsafed to justify His conduct, we are told, "His mother kept all these sayings in her heart."[45] And accordingly, at the marriage-feast in Cana, her faith anticipated His first miracle, and she said to the servants, "Whatsoever He saith unto you, do it."[46]

3. Thus St. Mary is our pattern of Faith, both in the reception and in the study of Divine Truth. She does not think it enough to accept, she dwells upon it; not enough to possess, she uses it; not enough to assent, she develops it; not enough to submit the Reason, she reasons upon it; not indeed reasoning first, and

---

42. Luke 1:38.
43. Luke 1:42–45.
44. Luke 2:19.
45. Luke 2:51.
46. John 2:5.

believing afterwards, with Zacharias, yet first believing without reasoning, next from love and reverence, reasoning after believing. And thus she symbolizes to us, not only the faith of the unlearned, but of the doctors of the Church also, who have to investigate, and weigh, and define, as well as to profess the Gospel; to draw the line between truth and heresy; to anticipate or remedy the various aberrations of wrong reason; to combat pride and recklessness with their own arms; and thus to triumph over the sophist and the innovator.

4. If, then, on a Day dedicated to such high contemplations as the Feast which we are now celebrating, it is allowable to occupy the thoughts with a subject not of a devotional or practical nature, it will be some relief of the omission to select one in which St. Mary at least will be our example — the use of Reason in investigating the doctrines of Faith; a subject, indeed, far fitter for a volume than for the most extended notice which can here be given to it; but one which cannot be passed over altogether in silence, in any attempt at determining the relation of Faith to Reason.

5. The overthrow of the wisdom of the world was one of the earliest, as well as the noblest of the triumphs of the Church; after the pattern of her Divine Master, who took His place among the doctors before He preached His new Kingdom, or opposed Himself to the world's power. St. Paul, the learned Pharisee, was the first fruits of that gifted company, in whom the pride of science is seen prostrated before the foolishness of preaching. From his day to this the Cross has enlisted under its banner all those great endowments of mind, which in former times had been expended on vanities, or dissipated in doubt and speculation. Nor was it long before the schools of heathenism took the alarm, and manifested an unavailing jealousy of the new doctrine, which was robbing them of their most hopeful disciples. They had hitherto taken for granted that the natural home of the Intellect

was the Garden or the Porch; and it reversed their very first principles to be called on to confess, what yet they could not deny,
that a Superstition, as they considered it, was attracting to itself
all the energy, the keenness, the originality, and the eloquence of
the age. But these aggressions upon heathenism were only the
beginning of the Church's conquests; in the course of time the
whole mind of the world, as I may say, was absorbed into the
philosophy of the Cross, as the element in which it lived, and the
form upon which it was molded. And how many centuries did
this endure, and what vast ruins still remain of its dominion! In
the capitals of Christendom the high cathedral and the perpetual
choir still witness to the victory of Faith over the world's power.
To see its triumph over the world's wisdom, we must enter those
solemn cemeteries in which are stored the relics and the monu-
ments of ancient Faith — our libraries. Look along their shelves,
and every name you read there is, in one sense or other, a trophy
set up in record of the victories of Faith. How many long lives,
what high aims, what single-minded devotion, what intense contemplation, what fervent prayer, what deep erudition, what un-
tiring diligence, what toilsome conflicts has it taken to establish
its supremacy! This has been the object which has given meaning to the life of Saints, and which is the subject-matter of their
history. For this they have given up the comforts of earth and
the charities of home, and surrendered themselves to an austere
rule, nay, even to confessorship and persecution, if so be they
could make some small offering, or do some casual service, or
provide some additional safeguard toward the great work which
was in progress. This has been the origin of controversies, long
and various, yes, and the occasion of much infirmity, the test of
much hidden perverseness, and the subject of much bitterness
and tumult. The world has been moved in consequence of it,
populations excited, leagues and alliances formed, kingdoms lost
and won: and even zeal, when excessive, evinced a sense of its

preciousness; nay, even rebellions in some sort did homage to it, as insurgents imply the actual sovereignty of the power which they are assailing. Meanwhile the work went on, and at length a large fabric of divinity was reared, irregular in its structure, and diverse in its style, as beseemed the slow growth of centuries; nay, anomalous in its details, from the peculiarities of individuals, or the interference of strangers, but still, on the whole, the development of an idea, and like itself, and unlike anything else, its most widely-separated parts having relations with each other, and betokening a common origin.

6. Let us quit this survey of the general system, and descend to the history of the formation of any Catholic dogma. What a remarkable sight it is, as almost all unprejudiced persons will admit, to trace the course of the controversy, from its first disorders to its exact and determinate issue. Full of deep interest, to see how the great idea takes hold of a thousand minds by its living force, and will not be ruled or stinted, but is "like a burning fire," as the Prophet speaks, "shut up" within them, till they are "weary of forbearing, and cannot stay," and grows in them, and at length is born through them, perhaps in a long course of years, and even successive generations; so that the doctrine may rather be said to use the minds of Christians, than to be used by them. Wonderful it is, to see with what effort, hesitation, suspense, interruption — with how many swayings to the right and to the left — with how many reverses, yet with what certainty of advance, with what precision in its march, and with what ultimate completeness, it has been evolved; till the whole truth "self-balanced on its center hung," part answering to part, one, absolute, integral, indissoluble, while the world lasts! Wonderful, to see how heresy has but thrown that idea into fresh forms, and drawn out from it farther developments, with an exuberance which exceeded all questioning, and a harmony which baffled all criticism, like Him, its Divine Author, who, when put on trial by

the Evil One, was but fortified by the assault, and is ever justified in His sayings, and overcomes when He is judged.

7. And this world of thought is the expansion of a few words, uttered, as if casually, by the fishermen of Galilee. Here is another topic which belongs more especially to that part of the subject to which I propose to confine myself. Reason has not only submitted, it has ministered to Faith; it has illustrated its documents; it has raised illiterate peasants into philosophers and divines; it has elicited a meaning from their words which their immediate hearers little suspected. Stranger surely is it that St. John should be a theologian, than that St. Peter should be a prince. This is a phenomenon proper to the Gospel, and a note of divinity. Its half sentences, its overflowings of language, admit of development; they have a life in them which shows itself in progress; a truth, which has the token of consistency; a reality, which is fruitful in resources; a depth, which extends into mystery: for they are representations of what is actual, and has a definite location and necessary bearings and a meaning in the great system of things, and a harmony in what it is, and a compatibility in what it involves. What form of Paganism can furnish a parallel? What philosopher has left his words to posterity as a talent which could be put to usury, as a mine which could be wrought? Here, too, is the badge of heresy; its dogmas are unfruitful; it has no theology; so far forth as it is heresy, it has none. Deduct its remnant of Catholic theology, and what remains? Polemics, explanations, protests. It turns to Biblical Criticism, or to the Evidences of Religion, for want of a province. Its *formulæ* end in themselves, without development, because they are words; they are barren, because they are dead. If they had life, they would increase and multiply; or, if they do live and bear fruit, it is but as "sin, when it is finished, bringeth forth death." It develops into dissolution; but it creates nothing, it tends to no system, its resultant dogma is but the denial of all dogmas, any theology, under the Gospel. No wonder it

denies what it cannot attain.

[...]

10. Theological dogmas are propositions expressive of the judgments which the mind forms, or the impressions which it receives, of Revealed Truth. Revelation sets before it certain supernatural facts and actions, beings and principles; these make a certain impression or image upon it; and this impression spontaneously, or even necessarily, becomes the subject of reflection on the part of the mind itself, which proceeds to investigate it, and to draw it forth in successive and distinct sentences. Thus the Catholic doctrine of Original Sin, or of Sin after Baptism, or of the Eucharist, or of Justification, is but the expression of the inward belief of Catholics on these several points, formed upon an analysis of that belief. Such, too, are the high doctrines with which I am especially concerned.

[...]

23. Particular propositions, then, which are used to express portions of the great idea vouchsafed to us, can never really be confused with the idea itself which all such propositions taken together can but reach, and cannot exceed. As definitions are not intended to go beyond their subject, but to be adequate to it, so the dogmatic statements of the Divine Nature used in our confessions, however multiplied, cannot say more than is implied in the original idea, considered in its completeness, without the risk of heresy. Creeds and dogmas live in the one idea which they are designed to express, and which alone is substantive; and are necessary only because the human mind cannot reflect upon that idea, except piecemeal, cannot use it in its oneness and entireness, nor without resolving it into a series of aspects and relations. And in matter of fact these expressions are never equivalent to it; we are able, indeed, to define the creations of our own minds, for they are what we make them and nothing else; but it were as easy to create what is real as to define it; and thus

the Catholic dogmas are, after all, but symbols of a Divine fact, which, far from being compassed by those very propositions, would not be exhausted, nor fathomed, by a thousand.

Poems & Hymns

The Pillar of the Cloud (Lead Kindly Light)

LEAD, Kindly Light, amid the encircling gloom
    Lead Thou me on!
The night is dark, and I am far from home —
    Lead Thou me on!
Keep Thou my feet; I do not ask to see
The distant scene — one step enough for me.

I was not ever thus, nor pray'd that Thou
    Shouldst lead me on.
I loved to choose and see my path, but now
    Lead Thou me on!
I loved the garish day, and, spite of fears,
Pride ruled my will: remember not past years.

So long Thy power hath blest me, sure it still
    Will lead me on,
O'er moor and fen, o'er crag and torrent, till
    The night is gone;
And with the morn those angel faces smile
Which I have loved long since, and lost awhile.

At Sea.
June 16, 1833.

Consolation
"It is I; be not afraid."

WHEN I sink down in gloom or fear,
    Hope blighted or delay'd,
Thy whisper, Lord, my heart shall cheer,
    "'Tis I; be not afraid!"

Or, startled at some sudden blow,
    If fretful thoughts I feel,
"Fear not, it is but I!" shall flow,
    As balm my wound to heal.

Nor will I quit Thy way, though foes
    Some onward pass defend;
From each rough voice the watchword goes,
    "Be not afraid! ... a friend!"

And oh! when judgment's trumpet clear
    Awakes me from the grave,
Still in its echo may I hear,
    "'Tis Christ; He comes to save."

At Sea.
June 23, 1833.

The Brand of Cain
I BEAR upon my brow the sign
    Of sorrow and of pain;
Alas! no hopeful cross is mine,
    It is the brand of Cain.

The course of passion, and the fret
  Of godless hope and fear, —
Toil, care, and guilt, — their hues have set,
  And fix'd their sternness there.

Saviour! wash out the imprinted shame;
  That I no more may pine,
Sin's martyr, though not meet to claim
  Thy cross, a saint of Thine.

Oxford.
November 18, 1832.

Private Judgment

POOR wand'rers, ye are sore distress'd
To find that path which Christ has bless'd,
  Track'd by His saintly throng;
Each claims to trust his own weak will,
Blind idol! — so ye languish still,
  All wranglers and all wrong.

He saw of old, and met your need,
Granting you prophets of His creed,
  The throes of fear to swage;
They fenced the rich bequest He made,
And sacred hands have safe convey'd
  Their charge from age to age.

Wand'rers! come home! obey the call!
A Mother pleads, who ne'er let fall
  One grain of Holy Truth;
Warn you and win she shall and must,

For now she lifts her from the dust,
　To reign as in her youth.

Off Cape Ortegal.
December 11, 1832.

The Age to Come

WHEN I would search the truths that in me burn,
　And mould them into rule and argument,
A hundred reasoners cried, — "Hast thou to learn
　Those dreams are scatter'd now, those fires are
　　spent?"
And, did I mount to simpler thoughts, and try
Some theme of peace, 'twas still the same reply.

Perplex'd, I hoped my heart was pure of guile,
　But judged me weak in wit, to disagree;
But now, I see that men are mad awhile,
　'Tis the old history — Truth without a home,
Despised and slain, then rising from the tomb.

Palermo.
June 9, 1833.

Desolation

O, SAY not thou art left of God,
　Because His tokens in the sky
Thou canst not read: this earth He trod
　To teach thee He was ever nigh.

He sees, beneath the fig-tree green,

Nathaniel con His sacred lore;
Shouldst thou thy chamber seek, unseen,
  He enters through the unopen'd door.

And when thou liest, by slumber bound,
  Outwearied in the Christian fight,
In glory, girt with Saints around,
  He stands above thee through the night.

When friends to Emmaus bend their course,
  He joins, although He holds their eyes:
Or, shouldst thou feel some fever's force,
  He takes thy hand, He bids thee rise.

Or on a voyage, when calms prevail,
  And prison thee upon the sea,
He walks the wave, He wings the sail,
  The shore is gain'd, and thou art free.

Off Sardinia.
June 18, 1833.

The Month of Mary

GREEN are the leaves, and sweet the flowers,
  And rich the hues of May;
We see them in the gardens round,
  And market-paniers gay:
And e'en among our streets, and lanes,
  And alleys, we descry,
By fitful gleams, the fair sunshine,
  The blue transparent sky.

Chorus.
O Mother maid, be thou our aid,
  Now in the opening year;
Lest sights of earth to sin give birth,
  And bring the tempter near.

Green is the grass, but wait awhile,
  'Twill grow, and then will wither;
The flowrets, brightly as they smile,
  Shall perish altogether:
The merry sun, you sure would say,
  It ne'er could set in gloom;
But earth's best joys have all an end,
  And sin, a heavy doom.

Chorus.
But Mother maid, thou dost not fade;
  With stars above thy brow,
And the pale moon beneath thy feet,
  For ever throned art thou.

The green green grass, the glittering grove,
  The heaven's majestic dome,
They image forth a tenderer bower,
  A more refulgent home;
They tell us of that Paradise
  Of everlasting rest,
And that high Tree, all flowers and fruit,
  The sweetest, yet the best.

Chorus.
O Mary, pure and beautiful,
  Thou art the Queen of May;

Our garlands wear about thy hair,
   And they will ne'er decay.

The Oratory.
1850.

The Two Worlds

UNVEIL, O Lord, and on us shine
   In glory and in grace;
This gaudy world grows pale before
   The beauty of Thy face.

Till Thou art seen, it seems to be
   A sort of fairy ground,
Where suns unsetting light the sky,
   And flowers and fruits abound.

But when Thy keener, purer beam
   Is pour'd upon our sight,
It loses all its power to charm,
   And what was day is night.

Its noblest toils are then the scourge
   Which made Thy blood to flow;
Its joys are but the treacherous thorns
   Which circled round Thy brow.

And thus, when we renounce for Thee
   Its restless aims and fears,
The tender memories of the past,
   The hopes of coming years,

Poor is our sacrifice, whose eyes
    Are lighted from above;
We offer what we cannot keep,
    What we have ceased to love.

The Oratory.
1862.

Part IV
Meditations

Hope in God — Creator

I.

1. God has created all things for good; all things for their greatest good; everything for its own good. What is the good of one is not the good of another; what makes one man happy would make another unhappy. God has determined, unless I interfere with His plan, that I should reach that which will be my greatest happiness. He looks on me individually, He calls me by my name, He knows what I can do, what I can best be, what is my greatest happiness, and He means to give it me.

2. God knows what is my greatest happiness, but I do not. There is no rule about what is happy and good; what suits one would not suit another. And the ways by which perfection is reached vary very much; the medicines necessary for our souls are very different from each other. Thus God leads us by strange ways; we know He wills our happiness, but we neither know

what our happiness is, nor the way. We are blind; left to ourselves we should take the wrong way; we must leave it to Him.

3. Let us put ourselves into His hands, and not be startled though He leads us by a strange way, a *mirabilis via*, as the Church speaks. Let us be sure He will lead us right, that He will bring us to that which is, not indeed what *we* think best, nor what is best for another, but what is best for us.

Colloquy. O, my God, I will put myself without reserve into Thy hands. Wealth or woe, joy or sorrow, friends or bereavement, honor or humiliation, good report or ill report, comfort or discomfort, Thy presence or the hiding of Thy countenance, all is good if it comes from Thee. Thou art wisdom and Thou art love — what can I desire more? Thou hast led me in Thy counsel, and with glory hast Thou received me. What have I in heaven, and apart from Thee what want I upon earth? My flesh and my heart faileth: but God is the God of my heart, and my portion for ever.

II.

1. God was all-complete, all-blessed in Himself; but it was His will to create a world for His glory. He is Almighty, and might have done all things Himself, but it has been His will to bring about His purposes by the beings He has created. We are all created to His glory — we are created to do His will. I am created to do something or to be something for which no one else is created; I have a place in God's counsels, in God's world, which no one else has; whether I be rich or poor, despised or esteemed by man, God knows me and calls me by my name.

2. God has created me to do Him some definite service; He has committed some work to me which He has not committed to another. I have my mission — I never may know it in this life, but I shall be told it in the next. Somehow I am necessary for His purposes, as necessary in my place as an Archangel in his — if, indeed, I fail, He can raise another, as He could make the stones

children of Abraham. Yet I have a part in this great work; I am a link in a chain, a bond of connection between persons. He has not created me for naught. I shall do good, I shall do His work; I shall be an angel of peace, a preacher of truth in my own place, while not intending it, if I do but keep His commandments and serve Him in my calling.

3. Therefore I will trust Him. Whatever, wherever I am, I can never be thrown away. If I am in sickness, my sickness may serve Him; in perplexity, my perplexity may serve Him; if I am in sorrow, my sorrow may serve Him. My sickness, or perplexity, or sorrow may be necessary causes of some great end, which is quite beyond us. He does nothing in vain; He may prolong my life, He may shorten it; He knows what He is about. He may take away my friends, He may throw me among strangers, He may make me feel desolate, make my spirits sink, hide the future from me — still He knows what He is about.

O Adonai, O Ruler of Israel, Thou that guidest Joseph like a flock, O Emmanuel, O Sapientia, I give myself to Thee. I trust Thee wholly. Thou art wiser than I — more loving to me than I myself. Deign to fulfill Thy high purposes in me whatever they be — work in and through me. I am born to serve Thee, to be Thine, to be Thy instrument. Let me be Thy blind instrument. I ask not to see — I ask not to know — I ask simply to be used.

III.

1. What mind of man can imagine the love which the Eternal Father bears toward the Only Begotten Son? It has been from everlasting — and it is infinite; so great is it that divines call the Holy Ghost by the name of that love, as if to express its infinitude and perfection. Yet reflect, O my soul, and bow down before the awful mystery, that, as the Father loves the Son, so doth the Son love thee, if thou art one of His elect; for He says expressly, "As the Father hath loved Me, I also have loved you. Abide in

My love." What mystery in the whole circle of revealed truths is greater than this?

2. The love which the Son bears to thee, a creature, is like that which the Father bears to the uncreated Son. O wonderful mystery! *This*, then, is the history of what else is so strange: that He should have taken my flesh and died for me. The former mystery anticipates the latter; that latter does but fulfill the former. Did He not love me so inexpressibly, He would not have suffered for me. I understand now why He died for me, because He loved me as a father loves his son — not as a human father merely, but as the Eternal Father the Eternal Son. I see now the meaning of that else inexplicable humiliation: He preferred to regain me rather than to create new worlds.

3. How constant is He in His affection! He has loved us from the time of Adam. He has said from the beginning, "I will never leave thee nor forsake thee." He did not forsake us in our sin. He did not forsake me. He found me out and regained me. He made a point of it — He resolved to restore me, in spite of myself, to that blessedness which I was so obstinately set against. And now what does He ask of me, but that, as He has loved me with an everlasting love, so I should love Him in such poor measures as I can show.

O mystery of mysteries, that the ineffable love of Father to Son should be the love of the Son to us! Why was it, O Lord? What good thing didst Thou see in me a sinner? Why wast Thou set on me? "What is man, that Thou art mindful of him, and the son of man that Thou visitest him?" This poor flesh of mine, this weak sinful soul, which has no life except in Thy grace, Thou didst set Thy love upon it. Complete Thy work, O Lord, and as Thou hast loved me from the beginning, so make me to love Thee unto the end.

The Infinite
Perfection of God

Ex ipso, et per ipsum, et in ipso sunt omnia.[47]

1. *Ex ipso.* I adore Thee, O my God, as the origin and source of all that is in the world. Once nothing was in being but Thou. It was so for a whole eternity. Thou alone hast had no beginning. Thou hast ever been in being without beginning. Thou hast necessarily been a whole eternity by Thyself, having in Thee all perfections stored up in Thyself, by Thyself; a world of worlds; an infinite abyss of all that is great and wonderful, beautiful and holy;

---

47. "For from him and through him and to him are all things" (Rom 11:36, RSV).

a treasury of infinite attributes, all in one; infinitely one while thus infinitely various. My God, the thought simply exceeds a created nature, much more mine. I cannot attain to it; I can but use the words, and say "I believe," without comprehending. But this I can do. I can adore Thee, O my great and good God, as the one source of all perfection, and that I do, and with Thy grace will do always.

2. *Per ipsum.* And when other beings began to be, they lived through Thee. They did not begin of themselves. They did not come into existence except by Thy determinate will, by Thy eternal counsel, by Thy sole operation. They are wholly from Thee. From eternity, in the deep ocean of Thy blessedness, Thou didst predestinate everything which in its hour took place. Not a substance, ever so insignificant, but is Thy design and Thy work. Much more, not a soul comes into being, but by Thy direct appointment and act. Thou seest, Thou hast seen from all eternity, every individual of Thy creatures. Thou hast seen me, O my God, from all eternity. Thou seest distinctly, and ever hast seen, whether I am to be saved or to be lost. Thou seest my history through all ages in heaven or in hell. O awful thought! My God, enable me to bear it, lest the thought of Thee confound me utterly; and lead me forward to salvation.

3. *In ipso.* And I believe and know, moreover, that all things live in Thee. Whatever there is of being, of life, of excellence, of enjoyment, of happiness, in the whole creation, is, in its substance, simply and absolutely Thine. It is by dipping into the ocean of Thy infinite perfections that all beings have whatever they have of good. All the beautifulness and majesty of the visible world is a shadow or a glimpse of Thee, or the manifestation or operation in a created medium of one or other of Thy attributes. All that is wonderful in the way of talent or genius is but an unworthy reflexion of the faintest gleam of the Eternal Mind. Whatever we do well, is not only by Thy help, but is after all scarcely an im-

itation of that sanctity which is in fullness in Thee. O my God, shall I one day see Thee? What sight can compare to that great sight! Shall I see the source of that grace which enlightens me, strengthens me, and consoles me? As I came from Thee, as I am made through Thee, as I live in Thee, so, O my God, may I at last return to Thee, and be with Thee for ever and ever.

The Infinite Knowledge of God

*Omnia nuda et aperta sunt oculis ejus; non est ulla
creatura invisibilis in conspectu ejus.*
All things are naked and open to his eyes; neither
is there any creature invisible in his sight.[48]

1. My God, I adore Thee, as beholding all things. Thou knowest in a way altogether different and higher than any knowledge which can belong to creatures. We know by means of sight and thought; there are few things we know in any other way; but

---

48. Hebrews 4:13.

how unlike this knowledge, not only in extent, but in its nature and its characteristics, is Thy knowledge! The Angels know many things, but their knowledge compared to Thine is mere ignorance. The human soul, which Thou didst take into Thyself when Thou didst become man, was filled from the first with all the knowledge possible to human nature: but even that was nothing but a drop compared to the abyss of that knowledge, and its keen luminousness, which is Thine as God.

2. My God, could it be otherwise? For from the first and from everlasting Thou wast by Thyself; and Thy blessedness consisted in knowing and contemplating Thyself, the Father in the Son and Spirit, and the Son and Spirit severally in each other and in the Father, thus infinitely comprehending the infinite. If Thou didst know Thy infinite self thus perfectly, Thou didst know that which was greater and more than anything else could be. All that the whole universe contains, put together, is after all but finite. It is finite, though it be illimitable! It is finite, though it be so multiform; it is finite, though it be so marvellously skillful, beautiful, and magnificent; but Thou art the infinite God, and, knowing Thyself, much more dost Thou know the whole universe, however vast, however intricate and various, and all that is in it.

3. My great God, Thou knowest all that is in the universe, because Thou Thyself didst make it. It is the very work of Thy hands. Thou art Omniscient, because Thou art omni-creative. Thou knowest each part, however minute, as perfectly as Thou knowest the whole. Thou knowest mind as perfectly as Thou knowest matter. Thou knowest the thoughts and purposes of every soul as perfectly as if there were no other soul in the whole of Thy creation. Thou knowest me through and through; all my present, past, and future are before Thee as one whole. Thou seest all those delicate and evanescent motions of my thought which altogether escape myself. Thou canst trace every act, whether deed or thought, to its origin, and canst follow it into

its whole growth, to its origin, and canst follow it into its whole growth and consequences. Thou knowest how it will be with me at the end; Thou hast before Thee that hour when I shall come to Thee to be judged. How awful is the prospect of finding myself in the presence of my Judge! Yet, O Lord, I would not that Thou shouldst not know me. It is my greatest stay to know that Thou readest my heart. O give me more of that openhearted sincerity which I have desired. Keep me ever from being afraid of Thy eye, from the inward consciousness that I am not honestly trying to please Thee. Teach me to love Thee more, and then I shall be at peace, without any fear of Thee at all.

The Providence of God

1. I adore Thee, my God, as having laid down the ends and the means of all things which Thou hast created. Thou hast created everything for some end of its own, and Thou dost direct it to that end. The end, which Thou didst in the beginning appoint for man, is Thy worship and service, and his own happiness in paying it; a blessed eternity of soul and body with Thee for ever. Thou hast provided for this, and that in the case of every man. As Thy hand and eye are upon the brute creation, so are they upon us. Thou sustainest everything in life and action for its own end. Not a reptile, not an insect, but Thou seest and makest to live, while its time lasts. Not a sinner, not an idolater, not a blasphemer, not an atheist lives, but by Thee, and in order that he may repent. Thou art careful and tender to each of the beings that Thou hast created, as if it were the only one in the whole world. For Thou canst see every one of them at once, and Thou lovest every one in this mortal life, and pursuest every

one by itself, with all the fullness of Thy attributes, as if Thou wast waiting on it and ministering to it for its own sake. My God, I love to contemplate Thee, I love to adore Thee, thus the wonderful worker of all things every day in every place.

2. All Thy acts of providence are acts of love. If Thou sendest evil upon us, it is in love. All the evils of the physical world are intended for the good of Thy creatures, or are the unavoidable attendants on that good. And Thou turnest that evil into good. Thou visitest men with evil to bring them to repentance, to increase their virtue, to gain for them greater good hereafter. Nothing is done in vain, but has its gracious end. Thou dost punish, yet in wrath Thou dost remember mercy. Even Thy justice when it overtakes the impenitent sinner, who had exhausted Thy loving providences toward him, is mercy to others, as saving them from his contamination, or granting them a warning. I acknowledge with a full and firm faith, O Lord, the wisdom and goodness of Thy Providence, even in Thy inscrutable judgments and Thy incomprehensible decrees.

3. O my God, my whole life has been a course of mercies and blessings shewn to one who has been most unworthy of them. I require no faith, for I have had long experience, as to Thy providence toward me. Year after year Thou hast carried me on — removed dangers from my path — recovered me, recruited me, refreshed me, borne with me, directed me, sustained me. O forsake me not when my strength faileth me. And Thou never wilt forsake me. I may securely repose upon Thee. Sinner as I am, nevertheless, while I am true to Thee, Thou wilt still and to the end, be superabundantly true to me. I may rest upon Thy arm; I may go to sleep in Thy bosom. Only give me, and increase in me, that true loyalty to Thee, which is the bond of the covenant between Thee and me, and the pledge in my own heart and conscience that Thou, the Supreme God, wilt not forsake me, the most miserable of Thy children.

Part V
Letters

Letters to Family Announcing His Election to Oriel College Fellowship, April 1822

The letters in this section commemorate Newman's
election as a Fellow of Oriel College, Oxford.
The letter to Charles describes the examination
process. The appointment was a milestone he
remembered throughout the rest of his life,
offering him a lifetime position of influence
and stature in the Church of England.

John Henry Newman to John William Bowden (friend)
April 12, 1822

My dear Bowden,
    I have just been nominated Fellow of Oriel College. —
Thank God
                    I am Yours most truly John Henry Newman

———

To Mr. Newman (Father)
April 12, 1822

    I am just made Fellow of Oriel. Thank God. Love to all.

———

To Elizabeth Newman (Aunt)
April 12, 1822

My dear Aunt,

   I have this morning been elected fellow of Oriel College. I do not know how sufficiently to be grateful to God for so great mercy — and my joy and thanksgiving are so much purer, inasmuch as I feel that what I have obtained *must* be good for me, for I have continually petitioned for *good*. — However great fortune is dangerous — pray for me that I be not puffed up or exalted above measure. Excuse great haste. With love to my dear Grandmother.

Believe me My dear Aunt Yours most affectionately
John Henry Newman

To Charles Robert Newman (brother)
April 13, 1822

Now that the contest and labour is all over, I may be allowed to state, that for the last month or two I have been so far from having a mean opinion of myself, which my Mother some how judged I had conceived, that I have actually considered myself as having a very good chance of succeeding, at the approaching examination. Instead of saying in the letter I wrote about six weeks ago, "*I* think I have no chance," I merely stated the opinion of everyone else.

   I am then fellow of Oriel; and, though unable at present to define the advantages that follow, I know enough to say with confidence and thankfulness that I have gained independence, competency, and literary society. Not that I expect any immediate emolument, but I have gained a spell which can conjure me as many pupils as I can desire.

I was not acquainted with a single fellow; my own College was rather undervalued; and the list of Oriel fellows contains the names of many first class men, and they obliged to stand a second year, while of Under-the-line men not one. The examinations commenced this day week (Saturday) — we were locked up for above 8 hours — on Monday above 9. on Tuesday about 4, and then brought up before the fellows for *viva voce*, which trial continued through Wednesday and Thursday. In the course of these days we had to do a Latin Essay, a translation of some Spectator, answers to twelve Mathematical and Philosophical, and to ten Logical Questions; besides construing passages in nine Greek and Latin authors before the Electors. There were ten candidates and two vacancies.

The examination throughout was most kind and considerate, and we were supplied with sandwiches, fruit, cake, jellies, and wine — a blazing fire, and plenty of time.

I think myself honoured inexpressibly by being among such kind, liberal, candid, moderate, learned, and pious men, as every act shows the fellows of Oriel as a body to be. There's a eulogium for you!

Yesterday I took my seat in Chapel, and dined with a large party in the Common Room. Today I have breakfasted and dined there, and shall in future, as a constant thing. I sat next Keble yesterday at dinner, and, as I have heard him represented, he is more like an undergraduate than the first man in Oxford — so perfectly unassuming and unaffected in his manner.

The confusion it has made in Oxford is very considerable; and my friends at Trinity were so kindly rejoiced that they could not read a word the rest of the day. Kinseey is in raptures, and Ogle declares that nothing has given him so great gratification since he came to his present situation, it being uncertain whether he means, since he took his first class since he became M.D., since he undertook the Tutorship of Trinity, or since he married

Mrs. Ogle.

The last Trinity man who got into Oriel was Dr Mant, about 14 years since.

I sent letters yesterday, besides home, to Bowden, Thresher, Dr Nicholas, and Aunt N.

Thus, not by the might of my arm, but by circumstances as seemingly unaccountable in themselves as those by which I lost my class, I am fellow of Oriel. I hope I have not been vain in any thing I have said. I am tied up at Oxford by my pupil, or I should like much to run up. I have not yet gone to the Bank about the money, for which thank my Father.

Keep this letter as I may wish to refer to it. Now indeed,

"I groan no more
Chained to the literary oar."

J H N

Debate with Charles Newman, July 26, 1825

The letter below is one of a series of exchanges
Newman had with his brother Charles over the
grounds for believing in the Bible and Christian
doctrine. The Newman brothers had very different
religious opinions and at times debated one another.

John Henry Newman to his brother, Charles Newman
July 26, 1825

My dear Charles,

You speak inconsiderately, when you express a wish "to hear
from me *shortly*," forgetting that I have many engagements which
employ my time. I felt it indeed a duty to engage in this corre-
spondence with you; yet there are other duties to which I have
more immediately dedicated myself, and which must have the
principal share of my attention. It has been my wish to reason
with you for your conviction rather than dispute for victory —
and with that view I have pointed out what I consider the error
in the inquiry you have been prosecuting, viz that you *did* decide
against Christianity FIRST from its doctrines and THEN *with this
prejudice against it on your mind* proceeded to examine the internal evidence of which in consequence you were no fair judge. I
have stated what I consider a *fact*; that your doubts of the truth of
Christianity *originated* in a dislike of its doctrines. I wished therefore to draw near and put my finger on the seat of the disease

— but, far from suffering me, you bid me keep my distance and prepare for action — Be it so — the mischief has been done, but tho' prejudice may have had great effect in forming your opinions, it cannot sharpen your arguments or blunt mine. I am not allowed to *convince* you, I must now attempt to *confute* you. —

The point I have maintained throughout, has been, that it is unfair to judge of the genuineness of a revelation by the things revealed — that its credentials are no more contained in the message itself which it purports to bring from heaven, than an ambassador's instructions from his sovereign are his credentials. To this you tell me you have replied in your MS. Almost the only sentence however which I can twist into even an allusion to it, is the following towards the conclusion: — "I think now (i.e. after attempting to account for the history of the Jews and the rise of Christianity on the hypothesis of an human original) I think now I have most fairly shown I am entitled to a hearing in the line of argument I am prepared to adopt against it" (Christianity) — that is, whereas *I* maintain you may not judge of its truth *from the doctrines it reveals, you* reply "having shown the *facts* which convey the revelation may be accounted for without the intervention of the Deity, I think I am fairly entitled to a hearing." This may be right or wrong, but surely nothing to the purpose. —

There is however another sentence at the opening of your MS, which is perhaps intended to bear upon the same point; and I would not deprive you of the advantage of it. *My* proposition (recollect) was, "you must not draw your arguments against Christianity from the doctrines, because, not being a fit judge of the truth or excellence of those doctrines, you cannot be sure your arguments are not fallacious." Your answer — "does it signify whence I draw my arguments, so that they are not fallacious?" Not at all — but if this is meant for a defence of your judging from the doctrines, it is just assuming the point in question. —

But since we cannot understand each other's meaning on the subject, I suppose I must pass from it — tho' to me the consideration of it is a full solution of the phenomenon of your present change of sentiment. Let me observe too you have not noticed my observations on the importance of praying for divine guidance in these difficult and momentous inquiries — observations not grounded on the precepts of Christianity, but on the natural feelings of every one who acknowledges a Providence, and confirmed by the actual practice of almost every country and age.

Debate with Francis Newman, October 22, 1840

In this letter, Newman was responding to a letter from
his brother Francis whose long religious journey had,
at this point, come to completion with the Unitarians.
Newman pushed back against Francis' rationalism.

To Francis Newman
October 22, 1840

My dear F,

Of course you can understand the pain your letter gave me,
without my expressing it. Not that I am surprised at what you
say of your present opinions; I was quite sure that you must
arrive at them one day or other, if you continued in your ad-
herence to those principles which for 14 years at least you have
held. Nay unless witheld by divine grace you must go further
still — your principles lead to scepticism on all points whatever, and this circumstance is to my mind a *reductio ad absur-
dum* of them. Whatever else is true, or false, man is made for
religion; and your principles make religion impossible. I am
not attempting to prove this; but I state my opinion for your
information, as you have stated yours for mine. And this I wish
you to understand of anything else I shall say.

I think your reasonings are irresistible, granting certain
latent principles which you all along assume. And since I anticipate that these will be generally assumed by the coming

age, as they are in great measure already, I am prepared for almost a downfall of Christianity for a time. Moreover do not let me hurt you if I say that in the plain and undeniable *irrationality* of the religion of the Church, on the assumption of the principles alluded to, I see a vivid exemplification of what the Apostle meant when he said that the worldly wisdom knew not God, and spoke of the preaching of the Cross as foolishness.

And what I have said will serve to explain my own conduct towards what you justly call the English way of handling the Evidences, Canon, proof of doctrine, etc. Considering that your conclusions are the legitimate issue of Protestant principles, when followed out, and that the English use and application of the latter is fallacious and ultimately untenable, I am not inclined to show mercy to what must one day be exposed and come to nought since it is better for men to be roused to a sense of their true state and to be shown whither they are drifting than to enjoy a hollow peace and dangerous rest some little time longer. Nor do I fear that such a course will eventually subserve your conclusions. Rather it will frighten men the other way. Latitudinarianism is an unnatural state; the mind cannot long rest in it; and especially if the fact of a revelation be granted, it is most extravagant and revolting to our reason to suppose that after all its message is not ascertainable and that the divine interposition reveals nothing. The more scepticism abounds, the more is a way made for the revival of a strong ecclesiastical authority; Christianity arose in the beginning, when the popular religions had lost their hold upon the mind. So strongly do I feel this, that, averse as the English people are to Romanism, I conceive that did their choice lie in the mere alternative they would embrace even Romanism rather than acquiesce in absolute uncertainty.

I have no fears then for the ultimate fortunes of Catholicism; I do but grieve and sigh over those who are destined to fall by the way in the wilderness ...

Regarding Newman's Conversion — To Simeon Lloyd Pope, September 18, 1845

Prior to his conversion, Newman wrote several
letters to friends and colleagues letting them
know that "something may happen." It was his
way of saying he thought he would soon enter
the Catholic Church. This letter to Simeon Lloyd
Pope was unique in that Newman outlined a
series of events that had led to his conversion.

To Simeon Lloyd Pope
September 18, 1845

My dear Pope,

I have long wished to know where you were, and now am
glad to see your handwriting, though on a painful subject. I write
to you at once.

It is now four years and a half, — since in a published Letter
to Jelf, — said that, if the English Church would keep certain
persons in it, she must tolerate their principles. This she has not
done — no one can be surprised at the consequence.

It is now near three years since I openly in print retracted
the harsh things I had said against the Church of Rome.

It is now two years this very day since I resigned St Mary's,
accompanying the act with a volume in which I clearly intimated

to any attentive reader what my state of mind was.

It is now a year nearly, since the strongest assertions were made in public by friendly writers about my intention, and half a year since they were made in public by my friends without any denial from me. I do not think any person has a right to be surprised.

But, my dear Pope, it is no motive of this world, such as the foregoing lines might seem to imply, which caused me to take this step. I am convinced that (*to those who* are enlightened see it) the Church of Rome is the only place of salvation. I do not think I can remain out of it, and yet remain in God's favor. This is no recent conviction. It is above seven years since I have professed in print Anglican doctrines — though I have since that done my best to support the Anglican Church — from a feeling that I had no right to decide hastily. I have given myself a very long probation, and meanwhile have tried to do my duty in that state in which I found myself. This is the issue. I shall give up my fellowship in the course of a month.

This Letter is in confidence

Ever Yrs affectionately John H Newman

Regarding Newman's Conversion — Letter from John Keble with Newman's Reply

This set of letters contains a letter Newman received from one of his greatest mentors and friends, John Keble (mentioned previously in the letter to Charles Newman from April 1822). Keble's letter to Newman was started prior to Newman's conversion, and then was completed after Keble received word that Newman had in fact left the Church of England for Rome. Keble's reaction conveys the great affection that many had for Newman and the great sorrow they felt at his conversion. Newman's reply was short, but conveys his admiration and appreciation for Keble.

From John Keble
October 3, and October 11, 1845

My dear Newman,

I feel as if I had something to say to you, although I don't very well know what it will be: but Charlotte's [Mrs. Keble's] illness having for the present at least abated, I find that I am better able than I have been for near a fortnight past to think and speak coherently of other things: and what can I think of so much as you, dear friend, and the great anxiety which awaits us with re-

gard to you: except indeed when my thoughts travel to Bisley to
Tom's bedside; for there as well as here everything almost seems
to have been, perhaps to be, hanging by a thread. At such times,
one seems in a way to see deeper into realities, and I must own
to you that the impression on my own mind of the reality of
the things I have been brought up among, and of its being my
own fault not theirs, whereinsoever I am found wanting — this
impression seems to deepen in me as Death draws nearer, and I
find it harder and harder to imagine that persons such as I have
seen and heard of lately should be permitted to live and die de-
ceiving themselves in such a point, as whether they are aliens to
the grace of God's Sacraments or no.

Oct. 11 at midnight. I had written thus far a week ago, and
then left off for very weariness, and now that I was thinking of
going on with my writing, I find that the thunderbolt has actually fallen upon us and you have actually taken the step which
we greatly feared. I will not plague you then with what I might
otherwise have set down — something which passed directly
relating to yourself in what fell from my dear wife on this day
fortnight, when in perfect tranquility and self possession, having
received the Holy Communion she took leave of us all, expect-
ing hourly to sink away. By God's great mercy she revived, and
still continues among us, with I trust increasing hopes of recovery; but the words which she spoke were such that I must always
think of them as of the last words of a Saint. Some of them I had
thought of reporting to you, but this at any rate is not the time.

Wilson has told me how kindly you have been remember-
ing us in our troubles: it was very kind, when you must have so
much upon your own mind. Who knows how much good your
prayers and those of other absent friends may have done us both
here and at Bisley? for there too, as I dare say you know, has
been a favourable change, and a more decided one, I imagine,
than here: at least their doctor has told them they may make

themselves comfortable; which is far beyond anything that has yet been said to us. But his recovery is very very slow. There too, as well as here, every thing has fallen out so as to foster the delusion, if delusion it be, that we are not quite aliens, not living among unrealities. Yet you have no doubt the other way. It is very mysterious, very bewildering indeed: but being so, one's duty seems clearly pointed out: to abide where one is, till some new call come upon one. If this were merely my own reason and feeling, I should mistrust it altogether, knowing, alas! that I am far indeed, from the person to whom guidance is promised, but when I see the faith of others, such as I know them to be, and so very near to me as God has set them, I am sure that it would be a kind of impiety but to dream of separating from them.

Besides the deep grief of losing you for a guide and helper, and scarce knowing which way to look — (though, I trust, thanks (in good part) to your kindness in many ways, I am not in so wretched a condition as I was) you may guess what uncomfortable feelings haunt me, as if I more than anyone else was answerable for whatever of distress and scandal may occur. I keep on thinking, "if I had been different, perhaps N. would have been guided to see things differently, and we might have been spared so many broken hearts and bewildered spirits." To be sure, that cold hard way of going on, which I have mentioned to you before, stands my friend at such times, and hinders me, I suppose, from being really distressed — but this is how I feel that I ought to feel, and I tell you and how I wish you to help me. That way of help, at any rate, is not forbidden you in respect of anyone of us.

My dearest Newman, you have been a kind and helpful friend to me in a way in which scarce anyone else could have been and you are so mixed up in my mind with old and dear and sacred thoughts, that I cannot well bear to part with you: most unworthy as I know myself to be: and yet I cannot go along with you: I must cling to the belief that we are not really parted; you have taught me so, and I scarce think you can unteach me. And having relieved my mind with this little word I will only say God bless you and reward you a thousand fold [for] all your help in every way to me unworthy and to so many others. May you have peace when you are gone, and help us in some way to get peace: but somehow I scarce think it will be in the way of controversy: And so, with somewhat of a feeling as if the spring had been taken out of my year,

I am always your affectionate and grateful, J. Keble.

To John Keble (in reply to letter from Keble dated following Newman's conversion)
November 14, 1845

May the Holy Trinity,
Father, Son, and Spirit,
    return to you sevenfold, My dear Keble, all the good, of which you have been the instrument towards me, since I first knew you. To you I owe it, humanly speaking, that I am what and where I am. Others have helped me in various ways, but no one can I name but you, among those I ever knew, except one who is gone, who has had any part in setting my face in that special direction which has led me to my present inestimable gain.

    Do not let me pain you, My dear Keble, by saying this. Let me not seem rude. Let it be your comfort, when you are troubled, to think that there is one who feels that he owes all to you, and who, though, alas, now cut off from you, is a faithful assiduous friend unseen.

Ever Yours very affectionately John H Newman

Letter of Condolence to Friend, Henry Bowden, Upon Death of His Wife, June 28, 1864

This letter is indicative of Newman's pastoral care.
Newman married Henry Bowden and his late wife in
1838 when they were all still Anglicans. Henry and his
wife became Catholics after Newman's conversion.

To Henry Bowden
June 28, 1864

My dear Henry,

We have been full of your great trial, and have said many
Masses for your dear wife, and for you, and all your children.
God has struck you most heavily, but your dear children will rise
up and console you. And God Himself, who has afflicted you,
will be your best Comforter and Friend.

She is now in peace and rest — for her great and long sufferings have been her deliverance from what she might have had
to suffer after death. For myself, thinking of her, this is a great
consolation. I feel that I have a great loss myself, the loss of one
so kind, so gentle, so open and true a friend, whom I sincerely
admired and loved, who talked with me so frankly and famil-
iarly, and made me know her by that most winning ease of her
conversation, — ah! it is a great distress to think I shall not see
her again, — but still to know that the worst is over, that all the

terrible suspense of pain and dying is ended, that she has crossed the awful river, this is to me a thought full of comfort. She cannot die again — she has heaven before her — O what a thought of peace is this! And you too, my dear Henry, must feel it, and you will feel it more and more. I doubt not you will be supported through your suffering, and learn to love God more and more, the more He afflicts you.

Thank you for the kind thoughtfulness of your letter — Your dear girls will let me know how you are.

Every Yours most affectionately in Xt
John Henry Newman of the Oratory

Regarding Newman's Role in the Church — Letter to Miss M. R. Giberne, February 10, 1869

Despite invitations and encouragements from friends (as shown in this letter) Newman did not attend the First Vatican Council. In this letter, he explains why he did not attend and describes himself in a way that paints an apt picture of his career.

Newman to Miss M. R. Giberne
February 10, 1869

My dear Sister Pia,

I wonder whether you have as mild weather in France as we have here. I am sitting without a fire from choice, nor have I had one, except in the evening, for nearly a week past. One does not know what it means. There may be subterraneous fires, which are doing their best to find a vent.

Thank you for all your prayers. I said Mass for you on the 28th and 29th January and should have written to you, had I not been busy.

Don't be annoyed. I am more happy as I am, than in any other way. I can't bear the kind of trouble which I should have, if I were brought forward in any public way. Recollect, I *could* not be in the Council, unless I were a Bishop — and really and truly I am *not* a theologian. A theologian is one who has mastered theology — who can say how many opinions there are on every point, what authors have taken which, and which is the best — who can discriminate exactly between proposition and proposition, argument and argument, who can pronounce which are safe, which allowable, which dangerous — who can trace the history of doctrines in successive centuries, and apply the principles of former times to the conditions of the present. This is it to be a theologian — this and a hundred things besides. And this I am not, and never shall be. Like St Gregory Nazianzen I like going on my own way, and having my time my own, living without pomp or state, or pressing engagements. Put me into official garb, and I am worth nothing; leave me to myself, and every now and then I shall do something. Dress me up and you will soon have to make my shroud — leave me alone, and I shall live the appointed time.

Now do take this in, as a sensible nun, and believe me

Ever Yours affly in Xt   John H Newman

Newman's Career Validated by Receiving Cardinal's Hat — Letter to Richard William Church, March 11, 1879

Rumors had swirled throughout England about the
possibility that Newman would be made a cardinal.
He was grateful for the honor after decades of trials
and difficulties. Writing to a close friend, Newman
unreservedly shared his gratitude and joy at the honor.

To R. W. Church
March 11, 1879

(Private)
My dear Church,

I did not like to write to you till I had something like official
notice of my promotion. This comes within this half hour. Yet
not so much official as personal, being a most gracious message
from the Pope to me.

He allows me to reside in this Oratory, the precedent for the
indulgence being Cardinal de Berulle, Founder of the French
Oratory in the 17th century.

Haec mutatio dexterae Excelsi![49] All the stories which have

---

49. Part of Psalm 77:10 from the Latin Vulgate. Full passage in the RSV: "And I say, 'It is my grief
that the right hand of the Most High has changed.'"

gone about of my being a half Catholic, a liberal Catholic, under a cloud, not to be trusted, are now at an end. Poor Ward
can no longer call me a heretic, and say (to H. Wilberforce) he
"would rather a man should not be converted than be converted by me —" and another writer give it as a reason why I was
not allowed to go to Oxford.

It was on this account that I dared not refuse the offer. A
good Providence gave me an opportunity of clearing myself of
former calumnies in my Apologia — and I dared not refuse it —
And now He gave me a means, without any labour of mine, to
set myself right as regards other calumnies which were directed
against me — how could I neglect so great a loving kindness?

I have ever tried to leave my cause in the Hands of God and
to be patient — and He has not forgotten me.

Ever Yours affly John H Newman

About the Editor

Matt Muller is an assistant professor of theology at Benedictine College and the associate director for programs for the Gregorian Institute at Benedictine College. He is also a board member for the Newman Association of America and an editorial board member for *Newman Studies Journal*. He holds a Ph.D. in historical theology from Saint Louis University. He has a Masters in Catholic Studies from the University of St. Thomas, in Minnesota. After graduating from Benedictine in 2006, he served for three years as a missionary with FOCUS at the University of Illinois. He and his wife, Jordan, have three children and reside in Atchison, Kansas.